BUILDING A CHURCH TO LAST

A Proven Model for Planting New Churches and Revitalizing Existing Ones

ROSS LINDSAY

FOREWORDS BY LUIS PALAU, J. I. PACKER, AND MALCOLM WIDDECOMBE

CONTENTS

DEDICATION

This book is dedicated to:

Charles Hurt Murphy, III, my pastor, my mentor, and my friend—a man after God's own heart

and

Ross M. Lindsay, Jr., my dad and my hero—a man who lives to pray

and

Jim Skinner, Phil Comfort, Bill Jones, Derek Tidball, Norman Doe, Linus Morris, Dwight Smith, and Joel Comiskey—godly men who have helped to build the Kingdom by sharing their lives and their intellects with their students

Foreword by
Dr. Luis Palau

I love the local church. Big or small, charismatic or conservative, the local church is one of the most important institutions – the only established structure – that Jesus left for us on this earth. It is His vehicle for ministry. It is his bride.

Today, local congregations are struggling. But in spite of their struggles, God has used some local congregations, like *All Saints, Pawleys*, in unique and powerful ways. He has taken these local congregations that have been ignited by His Holy Spirit and has used them to start incredible movements. That's why when I see great things taking place in local congregations, I get excited. It is proof that Jesus is continuing to work through us and through local congregations today in powerful ways!

BUILDING A CHURCH TO LAST is a *God story*—a beautiful example of what can happen when the Lord grabs hold of a small congregation and turns it on its head. It's a phenomenon felt not only within the four walls of a single church building, but also throughout the entire community and beyond. In the case of *All Saints, Pawleys*, it has led to further growth, further blessing, and further encouragement throughout the United States and the worldwide Anglican Communion.

I pray that you are blessed by this powerful story of restoration, growth, and new birth because the *All Saints, Pawleys'* story really offers encouragement to local congregations everywhere, regardless of their size, location, or affiliation.

Thank you, Ross Lindsay, for your diligent work in capturing this powerful story. I pray that this is just the beginning of great things for *All Saints, Pawleys* and for thousands of local congregations around the world whose leaders will read this book and implement the worship and leadership model that Chuck Murphy implemented at *All Saints, Pawleys*.

Luis Palau
Portland, Oregon
February 2011

Foreword by
Dr. J. I. Packer

L ying under the porch eaves in the warmth of the
Texas sun, the chrysalis, long inert, began to twitch.
I watched while, slowly and jerkily, with gaps during
which nothing seemed to be happening, it split open,
and through what looked like a struggle, the butterfly
emerged. Privileged to see what I saw, and delighting
in butterflies as I do, I was left with a deep-level thrill,
a glow of joy, and a song of praise in my heart. Yet
another miracle had occurred in God's glorious world.

Something comparable can happen in a previously
inert congregation when anointed leaders begin to link
vision with action. The resolve to move forward in a
fully biblical way takes hold. Worship becomes a united
quest for more of the God we serve as the Holy Spirit is
outpoured. Thankfully, I can testify that more than once
in my ministry I have seen this happen, and *All Saints,
Pawleys* is a case in point.

To tell the story of *All Saints, Pawleys*, in celebration of the work there and in hope of stirring other congregations and their pastors to seek a similar blessing
for themselves, is a service to us all. With sober preci-
sion, Ross Lindsay unfolds the narrative, and all who

long for God to show his hand more widely in our midst today will find it an absorbing page-turner. So read, meditate, enjoy, thank God, and be challenged! And may Ross Lindsay's book and the power of the Holy Spirit help to transform congregational potential into actual, free-flowing spiritual life in Christ, again—and again – and again.

J.I. Packer
Board of Governors' Professor of Theology
Regent College
Vancouver, Canada
February 2010

Foreword by
Canon Malcolm Widdecombe

*B*UILDING A CHURCH TO LAST is a learned work in which Ross Lindsay seeks to establish that the transformation that took place within *All Saints, Pawleys* was indeed a miracle. He draws heavily on the work of notable sociologists of religion, and, for me, his argument is quite convincing.

More than one miracle actually occurred at *All Saints, Pawleys* during *The Murphy Years* as Lindsay refers to them. It was an enormous privilege to read this book and also to discover along the way that I may have had a small role in the success that Chuck Murphy enjoyed during his tenure as Rector and senior pastor of *All Saints, Pawleys*.

I clearly recall that when Chuck Murphy did his practical work with me at Pip 'n' Jay in Bristol, England, I had the distinct feeling that he was extremely gifted and would do well in his ministry. Subsequent events have proved my estimation 100 percent correct. I am honored to be able to commend this book to my brothers and sisters in Christ in the U.S. and in the U.K. My sincere belief is that the first century worship and leadership model expounded upon in this book, if implemented, will enable any local congregation to experience the many blessings that *All Saints, Pawleys* has experienced.

With members like Ross Lindsay, it is no wonder that Chuck Murphy enjoyed the success that he obviously did at *All Saints, Pawleys*.

Canon Malcolm Widdecombe
Pip 'n' Jay
Bristol, England
March 2009

AUTHOR'S PREFACE

Miracle in Darien

In *Miracle in Darien*, Bob Slosser told the remarkable story of St. Paul's Darien, a tiny Episcopal church located in a suburb of Darien, Connecticut that became one of the fastest growing Episcopal churches in the United States after the Rev. Terry Fullam became its rector and senior pastor. Terry Fullam and the remarkable growth that occurred at St. Paul's had a significant influence on several Episcopal priests and congregations around the country, including the Rev. Chuck Murphy and All Saints Church in Pawleys Island, South Carolina (also known as *All Saints, Pawleys*).

In many ways, the story of *All Saints, Pawleys* is a continuation of the St. Paul's Darien story, but there is one key distinction. When Terry Fullam left St. Paul's, Darien, its attendance dropped significantly. The man and his charisma were gone, and many of the parishioners left the congregation. When Chuck Murphy left *All Saints, Pawleys*, its attendance did not drop because Murphy had put infrastructure in place to sustain it—a worship and leadership model that was described in the 2nd chapter of Acts. The remarkable growth at All

Saints was sustained by this "model," not by the charisma of Chuck Murphy.

The Murphy Years at All Saints, Pawleys

In 1982, the Vestry of *All Saints, Pawleys* called Charles H. "Chuck" Murphy, III to become its twentieth rector and senior pastor. Between 1982 and 2002, the average Episcopal church in the United States lost over 60 members. Between 1982 and 2002, *All Saints, Pawleys* gained over 600 members. I had the privilege of worshiping at *All Saints, Pawleys* during this twenty year period, and I witnessed first-hand the transformation of this tiny colonial congregation into an internationally recognized church.

During *The Murphy Years*, Chuck Murphy invited some of the best and brightest Anglican theologians to come to *All Saints, Pawleys* to preach and to teach. Before beginning his sermon, one of those guest preachers, the Rev. John Guest, stated: "It is such a privilege for me to preach at *All Saints, Pawleys*. Do you know that this church is one of only three Episcopal churches in the country that have grown ten-fold in the last ten years?" Those who worshiped regularly at *All Saints, Pawleys* knew that it was a special church, but few realized how fortunate they were to be worshiping in one of the three fastest growing Episcopal churches in the country.

Half-Time and my Second-Half Journey

One of the most profound books that I have read is Bob Buford's, *Half-Time*. As a successful attorney, CPA, and hotelier, I thought that I was living the dream. I suppose that I was to some degree, but Bob Buford challenged me to move from *success to significance* during my *second-half*. I now describe my second-half experience as moving from *empire building* to *Kingdom building*, but I had no clue how to begin the journey. So, I turned to my pastor, mentor, and friend Chuck Murphy, then senior pastor of *All Saints, Pawleys* for direction.

Murphy is a godly and gifted leader who served as the twentieth rector and senior pastor of *All Saints, Pawleys* until he was consecrated as one of the first missionary bishops *to* the United States by the Anglican Archbishops of Rwanda and South East Asia. He now serves as the Primatial Vicar for the Anglican Church of Rwanda and as the Chairman of the Anglican Mission in the Americas, a missionary outreach of the Anglican Church of Rwanda that has planted over 250 theologically conservative Anglican congregations in the United States and Canada.

Chuck Murphy's first recommendation for me was to improve my *head knowledge* of the Scriptures by enrolling in the Institute for Christian Leadership, a lay institute located on the campus of *All Saints, Pawleys*. I studied for three years at the Institute, at Trinity School for Ministry in Pittsburgh, Pennsylvania, and at Columbia Biblical Seminary in Columbia, South Carolina where I received an M.A. in Theology. Dr. Philip W. Comfort, the Dean of the Institute, and Dr. Bill Jones, the President of Columbia Seminary, encouraged me to continue my studies. So, I pursued and earned a Ph.D. in Church Growth from London School of Theology and an L.L.M. in Canon Law from Cardiff University Law School.

See It, Seize It, and Say It

Chuck Murphy once told me that I had a God-given gift: the ability to *see it, seize it, and say it.* This book is my attempt to do something *significant* during my *second-half* by telling the story of *The Murphy Years* at *All Saints, Pawleys*. I have tried to seize and say faithfully what I saw and experienced first-hand: the transformation of a small mainline congregation into a nationally and internationally recognized church.

If transformational growth can occur within a 250 year old mainline congregation like *All Saints, Pawleys*, it can occur in any congregation anywhere! My prayer is that other congregations will experience the same miraculous transformation that *All Saints, Pawleys* did by implementing parts if not all of the worship and leadership model described in this book. To God be the glory when they do!

Ross M. "Buddy" Lindsay, III
Pawleys Island, South Carolina
March 2011

1

Introduction

B ooks about how to *do church* more effectively have been best sellers in the Christian publishing industry for decades. An Internet search in early 2011 for books in print dealing with *church growth* revealed 6,642 titles in print including: *A Church for the 21st Century* (Anderson, 1992); *The High Impact Church,* (Morris, 1993); *The Purpose Driven Church,* (Warren, 1995); *The Missional Church* (Guden and Barrett, 1998); *ChurchNext,* (Gibbs, 2000); *The Church on the Other Side* (McLaren, 2000); *The Connecting Church* (Frazee, 2001); *The Emerging Church,* (McLaren, 2003); *Breakout Churches,* (Rainer, 2005); *Cell Church Solutions* (Comiskey, 2005); *Organic Church,* (Cole, 2005); *Simple Church,* (Rainer and Geiger, 2006); *The Living Church,* (Stott, 2007); *Tribal Church,* (Merritt, 2007); *The Blogging Church* (Bailey and Storch, 2007); *Comeback Churches* (Stetzer, 2007);*The Church of the Perfect Storm* (Sweet, 2008); *Sticky Church* (Osborne, 2008); *ChurchMorph* (Gibbs, 2009); *Deep Church* (Belcher, 2009); *Viral Churches* (Stetzer and Bird, 2010); *Transformational Church (*Stetzer and Rainer, 2010); and *Church 3.0* (Cole, 2010).

This Book Recommends a *Retrograde* for the Future of the Church

Neil Cole's excellent book, *Church 3.0* recommends several *upgrades* for the future of the church. Like Cole's book, this book is about transformational church growth, but it does not recommend an *upgrade* for the future of the church. Rather, this book recommends a *retrograde* for the future of the church—a return to the first century worship and leadership model that was used by the early church.

Why return to a first century model? Because the worship and leadership model used by the early church was highly effective, and the models recommended in the books listed above have achieved only limited success in both the United States and in the United Kingdom.

In 2009, the population of the United States was 307 million, and the inclusive membership in churches was 160 million.[1] The church in the United States had failed to reach 147 million people—48 percent of the population, in spite of the collective wisdom contained in the books listed above.

The Number of Unchurched People in America (and the U.K.) Is Increasing

When the Anglican Mission in the Americas (AMiA) was founded in 2000, Chuck Murphy stated that its mission was "to reach the 130 million unchurched people in America." In 2009, Chuck Murphy was still the Chairman of the AMiA, but the number of unchurched people in America had increased to 147 million.

According to the *2011 Yearbook of American & Canadian Churches,* inclusive church membership in the United States has *decreased* by over 1.1 million members during the last seven reporting years while the population has *increased* by over 19 million people.[2] These statistics have led church growth expert, George Barna to conclude that: "If the unchurched people in the United States were a nation unto themselves, that country would be the third most populated nation on the planet, behind only China and India."[3]

A More Effective Worship and Leadership Model Is Needed

The bottom line is that a different way of *doing church*—a more effective worship and leadership model—is needed, especially by congregations within the formerly mainline denominations in the United States and in the United Kingdom. This book sets forth such a model, not a new model, but the oldest known Christian worship and leadership model. The model is based on the worship and leadership practices that were used by the early church in the first century as they are recorded in the second chapter of Acts.

In order to prove the effectiveness of this first century worship and leadership model, this book presents a case study of an actual congregation that implemented the model—not just any congregation, but a 250-year-old mainline Episcopal congregation. If transformational growth can occur in a tiny mainline congregation located in the seaside hamlet of Pawleys Island, South Carolina, it can occur in any congregation that chooses to implement this model.

About this Book

Before describing the first century worship and leadership model in detail, Chapter 2 presents a more detailed look at the *State of the Church* and the crisis of faith and leadership that exists within it today. Chapter 3 highlights the findings of four comprehensive studies of congregational growth that confirm the need for a more effective model. Chapter 4 presents a biographical sketch of Chuck Murphy, the man, and an introduction to the first century worship and leadership model that he implemented at *All Saints, Pawleys*. Then Chapters 5 through 13 describe in detail the first century worship and leadership model that Chuck Murphy implemented at *All Saints, Pawleys*; and the final chapter presents some practical applications of the model.

The State of the Church: A Crisis of Faith and Leadership

A Gathering Storm Among the Churches

In 1969, sociologist Jeffrey Hadden described a gathering storm among the churches. According to Hadden, in the 1960s, the American mainline churches were being confronted by a threefold crisis: a crisis of meaning and purpose, a crisis of belief, and a crisis of authority. Hadden predicted that this deep and entangling crisis would eventually disrupt and alter the very nature of the church in the United States and throughout the world. Hadden further observed that many church leaders and the vast majority of the churchgoing public were not aware of the depth or the complexity of the growing crisis in faith and leadership within their churches.[1]

Almost forty years later, over 4,200 ordained and lay leaders of The Episcopal Church in the United States filled the Convention Center in Pittsburgh,

Pennsylvania for what was billed as the *Hope and a Future Conference.* The conference was hosted by the Rt. Rev. Robert Duncan, the Episcopal Bishop of Pittsburgh, and the Anglican Communion Network, an organization composed of theologically conservative leaders within The Episcopal Church who were seeking to return The Episcopal Church to its biblical roots. The delegates to the conference heard, many of them for the first time, that a crisis of faith and leadership existed within their church. Precisely what Jeffrey Hadden had predicted four decades earlier had become a reality in their church.

The State of the Church In the United States

According to the *2011 Yearbook of American and Canadian Churches,* during the five most recent reporting years, the largest protestant churches in the United States have lost collectively over 1.2 million members as shown in Table 1 below.

Table 1: Five Year Loss in Membership for Large U.S. Denominations

	Members	Percentage
Presbyterian Church (U.S.A.)	- 328,112	-10.5%
Evangelical Lutheran Church in America	- 307,908	- 6.3%
The United Methodist Church	- 300,079	- 3.7%
The Episcopal Church	- 241,476	-10.7%
Southern Baptist Convention	- 110,227	- .6%
Total/Average	-1,287,802	- 6.4%

Sources: *Yearbook of American & Canadian Churches: 2007, 2011.*

For perhaps the first time in its history, even the Southern Baptist Convention reported declines in membership for three consecutive years. The *2011 Yearbook* also reported that only five of the largest twenty-five churches in the United States experienced any growth in membership during the latest reporting year: Jehovah's Witnesses (2.0%), Church of God, Cleveland, Tennessee (1.76%), The Church of Jesus Christ of Latter-day Saints (1.71%), The Catholic Church (1.49%), and Assemblies of God (1.27%). All of the formerly *mainline* denominations experienced continued decreases in membership and attendance.

The State of the Church in the United Kingdom

Church membership and attendance have declined even more significantly in the United Kingdom during the last twenty-five years. According to the *U. K. Christian Handbook*, total membership in U.K. churches decreased from 7,553,346 to 4,372,260, or 42%, between 1980 and 2005, while average Sunday attendance at U.K. churches decreased from 6,021,600 to 3,976,060, or 33%, during the same period.[2] In the United Kingdom, as in the United States, the Anglican, Methodist, and Presbyterian churches have suffered the greatest membership losses.

Megachurches

Church growth experts are quick to point to Saddleback Community Church, Willow Creek Community Church, and other *megachurches* in the United States as notable exceptions to the general declines that have occurred in church membership and attendance. However, other experts have characterized the growth that has occurred within these large churches as "a mile wide but only an inch deep."

In 2007, Willow Creek Community Church released the results of a multi-year study that confirmed the validity of at least some of the criticism that has been leveled at the *megachurches*. Bill Hybels, Willow Creek's senior pastor, described the findings as "ground-breaking and earth-shaking," and added:

> Some of the stuff that we have put millions of dollars into . . . wasn't helping people very much. . . . Our dream now is to fundamentally change the way we do church . . . to really discover what God is doing and how he's asking us to transform the planet. . . . . We need to wipe the slate clean and start over.[3]

Hybels is to be commended for his forthrightness in commissioning this study and for disclosing its findings. However, he and Willow Creek do not need to wipe the slate clean and start over. They simply need to embrace and implement a different worship and leadership model, one that was used effectively by the early church and is being used effectively today in local congregations like *All Saints, Pawleys* in the United States and *Pip 'n' Jay* in Bristol, England. A few vibrant mainline congregations still exist in both the United States and the United Kingdom. Church growth experts sometimes refer to these unique congregations as *new paradigm churches.*

New Paradigm Churches
Donald Miller, Professor of Religion at the University of Southern California, has studied church growth in the United States and globally. In *Reinventing American Protestantism: Christianity in the New Millennium,* Miller, a liberal Episcopalian, observed that a revolution is slowly transforming American Protestantism.

According to Miller, a new style of Christianity is being born, and he has found some *new paradigm churches* that are changing the way that Christianity looks and is experienced in the United States. Miller has observed that these *new paradigm churches* are growing because they are providing a deep encounter with the sacred, an experience of the Holy Spirit. He described the *new paradigm churches* this way:

New paradigm churches eliminate many of the inefficiencies of bureaucratized religion by an appeal to the first-century model of Christianity . . . . This worship and the corresponding message provide direct access to an experience of the sacred, which has the potential of transforming people's lives by addressing their deepest personal needs.[4]

According to Miller, if the mainline churches are going to be revitalized, they must do two things. First, they must give the ministry back to the people. They must flatten their hierarchical structures. Second, the mainline churches must become vehicles for people to access the sacred in profound and life-changing ways. They need to create an environment where people actually encounter God. Miller calls this democratizing access to the sacred, making the sacred available to all, regardless of theological education and training.

Miller cited the *Vineyard Fellowship* churches as an example of *new paradigm churches.* According to Miller, the teaching and preaching at *Vineyard* churches remain theologically conservative, but the boundaries are more permeable and tolerant of varied lifestyles. Some church growth experts have questioned whether the *Vineyard* style of worship would appeal to members of a typical mainline church in the United States or the United Kingdom. Miller would say yes and offered this quote from the pastor of a *Vineyard* congregation in El Paso, Texas as proof:

> Our greatest success was with the . . . Episcopalians across town. They started coming to the Bible studies, and they wanted more of the Lord, more of the Holy Spirit. One night eighty of them showed up, including the rector. . . . It revolutionized this Episcopal church, so they in turn went out and planted another church. It was just awesome.[5]

Todd Hunter, one of the founders of the *Vineyard Fellowship*, was consecrated recently as an Anglican Bishop. Hunter describes what he calls the surprising appeal of the *liturgical* church in his book, *The Accidental Anglican.*[6] Hunter and Ellis Brust, the former CEO of the Anglican Mission in the Americas (AMiA) have begun planting 100 *new paradigm churches* in Southern California. Dave Roseberry, rector and senior pastor of *Christ Church, Plano* Texas, the largest Anglican congregation in the United States, is leading a movement sponsored by the Anglican Church in North America (ACNA) to plant 1,000 *new paradigm churches* throughout the United States. So, the *Vineyard* style of worship has begun to infiltrate the mainline churches in the U.S. and presumably in the U.K. as well.

A New Day is Dawning for the Protestant Church

Eddie Gibbs, an Anglican missiologist at Fuller Seminary in California, agrees with Donald Miller that a new day is dawning for the Protestant church in the United States. In, *ChurchNext* and *ChurchMorph,* Gibbs observes that the 21st century church is faced with a generation of under-thirty-five-year-olds who are turning away from institutional expressions of Christianity. According to Gibbs, the most helpful church models for reaching this generation are those that were utilized by the early church. Gibbs added:

Fortunately, the scene is not all gloom and doom. For at the same time that we see the demise of one section of the church, we see the flowering of another. . . . We are in the midst of a new reformation in American Protestantism. . . . where leadership will have to be apostolic, not bureaucratic . . . . [where] church planting needs to be given high priority by old-line denominations.[7]

Gibbs agrees with Donald Miller that radical changes need to be made also in seminary education. He recommends that local churches and the seminaries be brought together in a partnership of life-long learning and equipping, and he also advocates the creation of *lay institutes*. The Institute for Christian Leadership at *All Saints, Pawleys* was precisely that and will be discussed later in this book. Eddie Gibbs described *new paradigm churches* as local congregations that:

1. Recognize the centrality of worship.
2. Emphasize the transformational encounter with the living God.
3. Equip the people of God for mission in the world.
4. Empower emerging leaders.
5. Exude authority and assurance that the presence of the Lord is with them.[8]

According to Miller and Gibbs, the Protestant churches in the United States and the United Kingdom can survive and prosper, but only if they are *rein-*

vented—if a paradigm shift can occur in their worship and leadership models. They must return to the first century church model of worship and leadership. They must be transformed into *new paradigm churches.*

The Next Reformation

Statistics concerning the state of the church, like those presented earlier in this chapter, have led some church growth experts to conclude that little hope remains for the once thriving mainline denominations in the United States and the established churches in Europe. In 2005, Father John McCloskey, a notable Catholic priest in the Washington, D.C. area, made this prescient observation:

> The mainstream Protestants are losing left, right, and center. They have absolutely no impact and little remaining pulse. The upcoming 500th anniversary of the beginning of the Reformation, [2017], will show, I think, that mainstream Protestantism in any culture transforming sense is finished in America.[9]

Kevin Donlon, an Oxford trained church historian and canon lawyer, observed that reformations have occurred within the church every five hundred years since its inception, and 2017 will mark the 500th anniversary of the last reformation. Pastor Rick Warren of *Saddleback Church* declared at the Hope and the Future Conference in Pittsburgh in 2007 that the next reformation had already begun.

If the church as we know it is going to survive and thrive for another five hundred years, then local congregations, not national church bureaucracies, are going to have to man the frontlines. The goal of this book is to give pastors, church planters, and lay-leaders an effective tool to better equip themselves for the spiritual warfare that lies ahead.

The worship and leadership model described in this book is not a new and improved way of *doing church* in the 21st century. Rather, it is the proven and effective worship and leadership model of the early church that is described in the book of Acts. In the second chapter of Acts, God gave us the blueprints for building an effective church. What the 21st century church needs is pastors, church planters, and lay-leaders who are willing to pick up these blueprints and use them to rebuild His church.

3

Four Recent Studies Confirm the Need for a More Effective Worship and Leadership Model

The perfect storm that the church has confronted since the mid 1960s has thrust church growth and decline onto the radar screens of academicians as well as theologians and church growth experts. In 1979, two sociologists of religion, Dean Hoge and David Roozen reported the findings of a landmark study of church growth and decline that was commissioned and funded by several mainline denominations.

These social scientists concluded that *local contextual factors*, things that the churches had no control over, were causing the massive declines in membership and attendance. However the study did identify ten *local institutional factors* that contributed positively to congregational growth.[1] Since Hoge and Roozen's study, several other comprehensive studies of congregations have been conducted. The findings of four of these studies will be highlighted in this chapter. Two of the studies were conducted by academicians, and the other two were conducted by theologians and church growth experts.

Chuck Murphy is a voracious reader, and during *The Murphy Years* at *All Saints, Pawleys* he read constantly. Rather than suggest to the members of the congregation that they read certain books (because he knew that most would not), Murphy condensed them onto one or two page handouts and discussed them during the adult class that he taught following the Sunday worship services each week. Therefore, in authentic Chuck Murphy fashion, this chapter condenses the hundreds of pages of findings from these four congregational studies into the following several pages.

The National Congregational Survey (NCS)

The first of the four studies was the National Congregations Study (NCS). According to sociologist of religion Mark Chaves, a major gap existed in the previous research on congregations because no one had researched a nationally representative sample of American congregations. To fill this void, Chaves pulled together dozens of scholars and religious leaders who combined their expertise to design a questionnaire that became a part of the annual NORC General Social Survey. The National Opinion Research Center survey achieved an 80 percent response rate and produced data from over 1,200 American congregations.[2]

Chaves reported the findings of the NCS study in his book, *Congregations in America*, and his key findings are summarized below.

Key findings of the
National Congregational Survey

1. Most American congregations are small. 59 percent have fewer than 100 regular participants.
2. About half of all church goers attend the largest 10 percent of congregations.
3. If all non-denominational churches were combined, they would constitute the third-largest denomination behind the Catholic and Southern Baptist churches.
4. Conservative denominations are losing fewer people to moderate and liberal denominations than in previous decades.
5. Evangelical (conservative Protestant) congregations have become firmly middle class.
6. Evangelical congregations are growing, but their growth is not sufficient to offset the losses occurring in liberal churches.
7. Total giving to local congregations, adjusted for inflation, increased 63 percent between 1968 and 1998.
8. There is a steady movement in Christian worship toward more enthusiastic and less ceremonial practices.

The Congregational Life Survey (CLS)

In another in-depth study of U.S. congregations, the Congregational Life Survey (CLS), over 300,000 worshipers from over 2,000 congregations in the United States completed a questionnaire during religious services. For this study, the NORC identified a random sample of congregations attended by individuals who participated in the NORC General Social Survey for that year.

According to sociologists of religion Cynthia Woolever and Deborah Bruce, the goal of the CLS was to provide congregational leaders with the type of reality-based organizational analysis that business leaders in growing, healthy, excellence-oriented companies find helpful.[3] Woolever and Bruce reported their findings in *A Field Guide to U.S. Congregations*, and their key findings are highlighted below.

As a research tool for this book, a survey almost identical to the one used in the U.S.Congregational Life Survey was given to the members of *All Saints, Pawleys* in order to determine how *All Saints, Pawleys* compared to the average congregation surveyed by Woolever and Bruce. The results of the U.S. Congregational Life Survey and those of the *All Saints, Pawleys* survey are summarized below. (See Appendix 4 for the *All Saints, Pawleys* Membership Survey Questionnaire).

**Key Findings of the
U.S. Congregational Life Survey (CLS) and
the All Saints, Pawleys Survey (ASP)**

	CLS	ASP
Age distribution of worshipers:		
15-24	10%	4%
25-44	30%	26%
45-64	36%	37%
Over 65	24%	33%
The median budget	$99,610	$1,697,000

Spent time in devotions most days	45%	63%
Identified definite moment of conversion	28%	76%
Thought the Bible should be taken literally	28%	63%
Experienced God during worship	81%	86%
Attended less than five years	34%	40%
Attended less than two years	20%	26%
What worshipers value the most:		
Traditional worship style	65%	60%
Preaching	40%	80%
Contemporary worship style	35%.	40%

When compared to the average congregation of the two thousand congregations included in the Congregational Life Survey, some distinctive characteristics of the *All Saints, Pawleys* congregation are readily apparent:

1. The average age of the members at All Saints, Pawleys was higher than that of the average congregation in the CLS. All Saints, Pawleys had 37 percent more members that were over 65.
2. The budget at All Saints, Pawleys was seventeen times greater than the budget for the average congregation in the CLS Study.

3. 40 percent more of the members at All Saints, Pawleys spent time in daily devotions.
4. Over twice as many felt that the Bible should be taken literally.
5. Almost three times as many could point to a definite moment of conversion. Twice as many placed a high value of preaching.

According to Woolever and Bruce, the strengths of the U.S. Congregational Life Survey (CLS) were that: (1) it utilized a large representative national sample; (2) it solicited the opinions of both leaders and worshipers; and (3) it included a broad range of denominations and faith groups. The same things could be said about Chaves' National Congregation Survey (NCS). The primary weakness of both the CLS and the NCS was that the studies revealed a profile for the *average* American congregation, not a profile for a growing, healthy, and excellence-oriented congregation in the United States, which was their stated goal.

The *Breakout Church* Study

A third and more recent comprehensive study of American congregations was conducted by Thom Rainer and a team of researchers from the Billy Graham School for Missions, Evangelism, and Church Growth at Southern Baptist Theological Seminary in Louisville, Kentucky. Unlike the CLS and the NCS, Rainer's study did produce the type of "reality-based organizational analysis" that many pastors and congregational leaders have long sought.

Thom Rainer and his research team reviewed data from over 1,900 American congregations in order to identify what they called *breakout churches*—churches that had shown historical attendance declines that were followed by at least five years of significant growth in worship attendance. Rainer's research team used the principles and findings discussed by Jim Collins in his book, *Good to Great,* to identify churches that had moved from *good to great.*

In *Good to Great,* Collins maintained that *good is the enemy of great.* In order to identify and study truly great companies, Collins studied 1,435 companies and found that only eleven of them met the criteria to be considered *great companies.*[4] Rainer and his team requested ten years of historical data from 1,936 churches and discovered that only thirteen of them met the criteria to be considered *breakout churches.* Once these thirteen *breakout* churches were identified, Rainer's research staff conducted follow-up telephone interviews and on-site studies. Rainer described the characteristics of the thirteen *breakout* churches in his book, *Breakout Churches: Discover How to Make the Leap.*[5]

Some of the common characteristics of the thirteen *breakout churches* and their pastors are summarized below.

Common Characteristics of Breakout Churches

1. The pastors did not lead by the force of a charismatic personality but possessed fierce Biblical faithfulness, compelling modesty, confident humility, and contagious optimism.
2. The pastors were quick to give ministry to others and to let them take the credit for the work.
3. The pastors had a long-term commitment to one church. The average tenure of the pastors in the thirteen breakout churches was 21.6 years.
4. The pastors tended toward slow progress. They were sensitive to criticism, but they did not let

their critics deter them from the vision they sensed God had given them.

5. The pastors had an insatiable appetite to learn and a persistent drive to improve.
6. The breakout churches were all outwardly focused and were intentional about evangelism.
7. All of the breakout churches and their leaders were evangelicals (conservative theologically) who believed in the truthfulness of Scripture, and they held to the priority of preaching and the primacy of prayer.
8. Breakout churches learned to act quickly and compassionately when a personnel issue became negative. The "team" concept was vital.
9. Breakout churches understood that members must get connected within a small group. Members involved in worship services alone tended to drift toward inactivity.
10. Breakout churches did not have difficulty finding staff. Qualified staff found them because of the excellent working environment that they had created.

Academicians may find some of Rainer's observations anecdotal; however, these observations will serve as an effective lens through which to view the transformational growth that occurred at *All Saints, Pawleys* as it implemented the first century worship and leadership model. *All Saints, Pawleys* met all of Rainer's criteria for being a *breakout* church. The *modus operandi* of *All Saints, Pawleys'* senior pastor, Chuck Murphy, was to *take a step and take a step,* slowly but *intentionally* moving the congregation toward its *preferred future.*

Chuck Murphy had served as rector and senior pastor for twenty-two years when he suggested that the Vestry begin the search process for his successor. Thus, Murphy's tenure was only slightly longer than Rainer's 21.6 year average tenure for pastors of *breakout churches*. Every one of Rainer's thirteen *breakout* churches considered themselves *evangelical* churches. This fact, coupled with data that Rainer has assembled about the unchurched in United States, has convinced him that *non-denominational, evangelical, community churches* are the most effective type of churches for reaching the lost—both the *previously churched* and the *unchurched*.[6]

The *Transformational Church* Study

In the most recent study, the largest research study of congregations ever conducted, Thom Rainer and Ed Stetzer conducted surveys of over 7,000 congregations in order to identify the top ten percent that met the qualifications of a *Transformational Church*. Ed Stetzer is missiologist in residence at LifeWay Christian Resources in Nashville, Tennessee. He is a widely published author and has served as an advisor on church planting to the Anglican Mission in the Americas since 2005.

After the top ten percent of the congregations had been identified, the researchers interviewed 250 leaders from those congregations. They also analyzed data from surveys of over 15,000 members from these top tier congregations. This analysis enabled the researchers to identify and describe several *transformational church principles*.[7]

In order to qualify as a *Transformational Church*, a congregation had to meet several criteria. First, a congregation had to have grown at least ten percent in worship attendance during the previous five years. Second, the congregation had to have a high percentage of its attendees involved in a Sunday school class or other small group. Third, the congregation had to have a high percentage of its attendees involved in mission inside and outside of the church.[8]

What Rainer and Stetzer discovered as they reviewed the data from the interviews and surveys was that the majority of the people in the majority of the congregations in the United States were *passive spectators* rather than *active participants* in the ministry and mission of God. The majority of the church members were not engaged in any type of meaningful ministry or mission inside or outside of the church.

Stetzer presented the findings of this study to over 1,400 Anglicans who attended the eleventh annual Winter Conference of the Anglican Mission in the Americas that was held in Greensboro, North Carolina in February 2011. According to Stetzer, "Our study concluded that the majority of the people in the majority of the congregations in America come to watch the show—to sit, soak, and sour—to pay, pray, and get out of the way, so that the paid professional clergy can serve them. They are *customers* rather than *co-laborers* for the cause of Christ."

All Saints, Pawleys met the criteria established by Rainer and Stetzer for a *Transformational Church*. Its rate of growth averaged 9.2 percent *per year* for the 22 years that Chuck Murphy was rector and senior pastor. Murphy encouraged the members to participate in small group Bible studies that met weekly in people's homes. In addition, there were fifty-six different lay ministry organizations that enabled attendees to participate in mission both inside and outside of the church. As a result, the majority of the members at *All Saints, Pawleys* were engaged in meaningful mission and ministry during *The Murphy Years.*

The Need for a More Effective Worship and Leadership Model

The researchers and the methodology of the four comprehensive studies of congregations highlighted above differed. Two of the studies were conducted by social scientists, and the other two were conducted by theologians and church growth experts. Yet, after reviewing the findings of all four studies, one can draw the same conclusion. Congregations in the United States (and in the United Kingdom) need a more effective worship and leadership model.

During *The Murphy Years* at *All Saints, Pawleys*, Chuck Murphy implemented such a model, a proven and effective model that was based on the worship and leadership methods of the early church as they are described in the second chapter of Acts. As Murphy began implementing the first century worship and leadership model at *All Saints, Pawleys*, a remarkable transformation occurred within this 250-year-old congregation. The next chapter introduces Chuck Murphy, the man and the model.

4

Chuck Murphy: The Man and The Model

Anglicans had been worshiping on what is today the campus of *All Saints, Pawleys* for over two hundred and fifty years when the Vestry of the congregation called Charles Hurt Murphy, III, affectionately known as "Chuck," to become its twentieth rector and senior pastor.

In 1982, when Chuck Murphy arrived in Pawleys Island, the population was 3,446, and the community had one traffic light that flashed caution after dark. Twenty years later, the population had increased to 10,309. When Chuck Murphy became the twentieth rector and senior pastor at *All Saints, Pawleys*, average Sunday attendance was approximately 75, which is typical for Episcopal congregations. Twenty years later, average Sunday attendance at *All Saints, Pawleys* had increased to over 800 making *All Saints, Pawleys* one of the largest Episcopal congregations in the country.

The news of the dramatic growth and transformation that was occurring at *All Saints, Pawleys* spread widely, and soon Episcopalians and Anglicans from all over the country and the world started coming to visit this unique church. Often, the first questions that they asked were: "Who is this Chuck Murphy? Where did he come from?"

Chuck Murphy—The Man

Chuck Murphy was born and educated in Alabama. His father was a professional musician prior to becoming an Episcopal priest. After completing five years of undergraduate studies (and partying, according to his wife, Margaret) at the University of Alabama, Murphy spent a year in banking, during which he contemplated a career in law or ministry.

According to Murphy: "I thought that I had the gifts and the skill-set to be successful as a lawyer or as a minister. I felt that I could entice people into the dance. I had watched my father do it for years, and I liked the results." So Murphy attended a diocesan discernment weekend that was sponsored by the Diocese of Alabama, and he scored the highest on the aptitude test for clergy of anyone in the history of the diocese. "This was very confirming for Margaret and me," Murphy said, "although Margaret was not really thrilled about becoming a preacher's wife."

The Rev. Tom Jones, an Episcopal priest in Alabama, introduced Chuck Murphy to the Rev. John Guest, an English priest who became, first the youth director and later, the Rector of St. Stephens Episcopal Church in Sewickley, Pennsylvania, a suburb of Pittsburgh. Guest also helped establish Trinity School of Ministry in Pittsburgh, Pennsylvania. Trinity Seminary has become one the last bastions of orthodoxy and evangelicalism within The Episcopal Church and annually sends theologically conservative graduates into Episcopal and

Anglican churches throughout the United States and more recently Africa.

Tom Jones and John Guest had studied under Dr. J. I. Packer at Tyndale Hall, in Bristol, England, and they encouraged Murphy to do the same. So Chuck Murphy attended Tyndale Hall where Dr. Packer served as his personal tutor. "It was an awesome experience," Murphy said, "because I got to sit with Packer, one on one, every Friday. I had to be prepared because, unlike in my undergraduate classes, I knew that I would be called on to answer questions about the material."

While Chuck Murphy was studying in Bristol, Tyndale Hall merged with Dalton House and Clifton to become Trinity College. According to Murphy, Dr. Packer was a classical evangelical; however, unlike John Stott and some of his Anglican contemporaries, Packer was much more receptive to the Pentecostal movement that was evolving within the Church of England at the time. Packer saw the hand of God at work in the Pentecostal movement.

In 1971, Packer sent Chuck Murphy into the inner city of Bristol to experience the worship at the historic parish church of St. Philip and St Jacob, also known as Pip 'n' Jay. Pip 'n' Jay had been a parish of the Church of England since at least 1174 when it was one of the fiefs of William, Earl of Gloucester. During the eighteenth century, Pip 'n' Jay had welcomed such noteworthy preachers as John and Charles Wesley and George Whitefield to its pulpit. However, following World War II, the size of the congregation declined rapidly.

The membership of the parish had dwindled to seventeen when the assistant curate, the Rev. Malcolm Widdecombe, began leading a small group of young people in enthusiastic worship on Sunday evenings. Widdecombe became one of the pioneers of the charismatic movement in England, and what Chuck Murphy observed at Pip 'n' Jay would become an integral part of his own worship style and ministry. According to Murphy:

> At Pip 'n' Jay, Malcolm Widdecombe was able to create a space and a place to encounter God, within the framework and trappings of the Anglican liturgy. The world was crying out for an encounter with God. It was longing for transcendence, and Malcolm opened a window to it in the classical Anglican liturgy. He was able to create an opportunity for his members to experience the transcendence of the living God.

Widdecombe and his wife Meryl continued to lead the worship at Pip 'n' Jay for over forty years until Malcolm's death in 2010. Unlike many Church of England services, the services at Pip 'n' Jay were always well attended by enthusiastic members from many nationalities and socioeconomic levels. When asked about his efforts to create a space within the Anglican liturgy for people to experience God, Widdecombe responded:

> The liturgy is not our master. It is our servant. We should enjoy it. After the benediction, we don't say amen; we shout and clap! There was a time when I couldn't stand the Pentecostals, then I became one.[1]

Following a well-attended Sunday evening worship service at Pip-n-Jay, the Widdecombes reminisced about their encounter with Chuck and Margaret Murphy. They recalled many late-night chats while the Murphys lived with them in the nine-bedroom vicarage for several weeks until housing became available at

Trinity College. "I knew that Chuck would do well," Malcolm said. "I asked him to give his testimony one night, and he did a splendid job. He preached his first sermon here too." Meryl said that she understood that Chuck Murphy had become somewhat of a maverick within the Anglican Communion. She added enthusiastically: "Chuck Murphy is a rebel because he was taught by a rebel."

J. I. Packer, Chuck Murphy's advisor at Trinity College, is presently the Board of Governors' Professor of Theology at Regent College, Vancouver, Canada. During *The Murphy Years,* Packer preached at *All Saints, Pawleys* on several occasions, and he always referred to Chuck Murphy as "one of my boys." However, according to Dr. Packer, Chuck Murphy was an average student with no particular agenda while he was at Trinity College. Therefore, he was pleasantly surprised to learn of Murphy's involvement, nationally and internationally, first in the affairs of the Episcopal Church, and later in the AMiA and the global Anglican Communion.

After spending a year at Trinity College under Packer's tutelage, Murphy had exhausted his savings. Thus, he and his wife, Margaret, returned to the United States, so that he could complete his theological education at Sewanee Seminary in Tennessee. The foundation in classical Anglican theology that Chuck Murphy had received at Trinity College did not mesh well with the revisionist theology that was then being propagated at Sewanee.

Chuck Murphy defines classical Anglican theology as *the faith once delivered to the Saints*, and he recalled his time at Sewanee with some angst. He noted: "I was deemed unteachable by the faculty and staff at Sewanee, but by God's grace, I graduated."

Not long after Murphy finished seminary, the Diocese of Alabama invited some of the best and the brightest professional fund raisers in the country to a symposium on stewardship for the clergy. According to Chuck:

> I was impressed with the fund raising tools and techniques that were presented by these experts, but I felt that the theology piece was missing. The professionals presented the concepts, but there was no teaching based on Scripture. I did not want to sell the concept to members. I wanted to explain it to them. I wanted them to understand the Biblical basis for giving. So, I devised my own apologetics, using Ezekiel 36 and Jeremiah 31, and they began to catch on.

Murphy's apologetics were so compelling that he began to receive invitations to teach stewardship at Episcopal churches around the country. He accepted many of these invitations, and the observations that he made while visiting the various churches proved invaluable to him in his later ministry. "I got to see the best parishes with the brightest leaders because they could afford me, and I got to see some of the worst ones because they desperately needed me. I was able to observe what these churches did well, and I also saw what they did pitifully." Murphy continued to teach stewardship to members of Episcopal congregations throughout the United States for fifteen years after he became Rector of *All Saints, Pawleys*.

Chuck Murphy's Early Ministry
Chuck Murphy's first assignment, after his ordination to the priesthood, was to serve as an Assistant Rector

at St. Paul's Episcopal Church in Selma, Alabama. Murphy alluded to the racial tensions that occurred in Selma in the 1960s when he observed: "Selma was actually a place, not just an event." After two years at St. Paul's, Selma, Chuck Murphy became the Rector of St. Thomas' Episcopal Church in Greenville, Alabama, where he served for three years.

"One day at St. Thomas, Greenville, while I was preparing to teach a Bible Study, the Holy Spirit revealed to me that the second chapter of Acts describes a model of Christian worship and leadership that has been abandoned by the Protestant church in the West." In order to communicate this concept to his members, Murphy constructed a wheel that contained eight spokes. According to Murphy, "These eight spokes (which he would later describe as eight building blocks) served as the essence of life in the early church: (1) the Word is proclaimed; (2) the need is acknowledged; (3) Baptism; (4) the Apostles' teaching, fellowship, and the Eucharist; (5) miracles, awe, and power; (6) the theology of stewardship; (7) the theology of worship; and (8) the importance of growth." During his ministry at *All Saints, Pawleys*, Chuck Murphy taught repeatedly these eight building blocks of life in the early church.

The Murphys and their three small daughters then moved to Columbia, South Carolina, where Chuck Murphy had accepted the call to serve as Canon Theologian at Trinity Episcopal Cathedral. Two years later, the Rt. Rev. FitzSimmons Allison, the Bishop of the Diocese of South Carolina, asked Chuck Murphy to consider becoming the twentieth rector of *All Saints, Pawleys*. Murphy enjoyed his time at Trinity Cathedral; however, his home was located in the suburbs, and the Cathedral was located in downtown Columbia which required a lengthy commute. In addition, Murphy found that Vestry and committee meetings were typically held in the evenings; therefore, he had very little time to spend with Margaret and his three daughters.

Chuck Murphy described his attraction to Pawleys Island this way:

> I am a workaholic, and one of the attractions of *All Saints, Pawleys* was its small setting. Since the rectory was literally across the street from my office, I had immediate access to my family. Of course, it was also a beautiful place, and I really felt called to serve there. Pawleys Island was becoming a retirement community, and people that retire can only enjoy so much golf and water. Sooner or later, they have a longing for the transcendent. Educated and affluent people from all over the country were moving to Pawleys Island, and they were longing for community, fellowship, transcendence—an encounter with the living God. I felt called to establish a place where they could meet God.

So, Charles Hurt Murphy, III became the twentieth Rector of *All Saints, Pawleys*. Murphy served as Rector of *All Saints, Pawleys* for twenty-three years. During the last five years, he wore two hats: he served as senior pastor of the local congregation, and he served as chairman of the Anglican Mission in the Americas, a missionary outreach of the Anglican Church of Rwanda whose headquarters were located on the campus of *All Saints, Pawleys*.

Chuck Murphy Arrived at *All Saints, Pawleys* in 1982

When Chuck Murphy arrived at *All Saints, Pawleys* in 1982, he immediately received the support of the matriarchs and patriarchs of the parish. According to Murphy, this "buy-in" from the old names, coupled with a steady influx of sharp outsiders, provided an ideal mix that he began to shape into a new paradigm church. Murphy recalled: "One of my first challenges was to teach my way out of the 'shepherd model' and into the 'rancher model' of congregational leadership."

The shepherd and rancher models had been introduced by Carl George, the Director of the Charles E. Fuller Institute of Evangelism and Church Growth at Fuller Seminary in California. According to George:

> [The shepherd model] makes the pastor available as the primary care giver to everyone who will respond. To become a rancher, [the pastor] must acknowledge certain realities: he cannot deliver help to all people at the levels they require. In short, I suggest a *changed paradigm* for church leadership, one that shifts from doing the caring to seeing to it that people get cared for, which means that you develop and manage a system of care giving that will include as many *lay leaders* as possible [emphasis added].[2]

Historically, Episcopal and Anglican churches have been clergy-driven. Lay involvement has been minimal. As Ed Stetzer likes to say: A clear distinction was made between duties and the responsibilities of the "ordained" and the "ordinary" members of the church.

Chuck Murphy Was a Rancher, Not a Shepherd

When Chuck Murphy began to teach his way out of the shepherd model at *All Saints, Pawleys*, he was able to rely upon the success of another Episcopal priest, the Rev. Terry Fullam, and his experience at St. Paul's, Darien. St. Paul's, Darien was located in Fairfield County, Connecticut, the wealthiest county in the United States. St. Paul's, Darien was a stereotypical Episcopal congregation until its Vestry called the Rev. Everett L. Terry Fullam to become its next rector. Fullam became one of the first Episcopal priests in the United States to implement Carl George's rancher model, and the results were dramatic. During Fullam's first five years at St. Paul's, Darien, average Sunday attendance increased from 200 to 1200.[3]

According to Chuck Murphy, the two keys to Terry Fullam's success at St. Paul's were his ability to teach and his ability to draw people into worship. Fullam would sit down at the piano and teach as he played praise and worship songs. When Terry Fullam retired, attendance at St. Paul's dropped precipitously. Fullam's assistants, Martyn Minns and Thaddeus Barnum, also left St. Paul's soon after he did. Chuck Murphy saw what happened at St. Paul's and was determined to put an infrastructure in place at *All Saints Pawleys,* that was not dependent on his persona or charisma. Murphy wanted to build a church to last, one that would continue to grow after his departure.

Therefore, armed with George's rancher model of church leadership, and aware of Terry Fullam's early success and later disappointment at St. Paul's, Darien, Chuck Murphy began to teach his way out of the shepherd model and into another model, the first century model of worship and leadership. According to Murphy, "In those early days, I invited Terry Fullam, John Guest, J. I. Packer, Michael Green, Francis MacNutt, and John Stone Jenkins to come to *All Saints, Pawleys* to teach and to preach in order to reinforce what I was teaching and preaching. I wanted the members at *All Saints, Pawleys* to know that these were not just my ideas."

As a result of Murphy's teaching, preaching, and visionary leadership, and this reinforcement from outside speakers, *All Saints, Pawleys* began to be transformed into a new paradigm church.

Attendance and Giving Increased Dramatically
After the First Century Worship and Leadership
Model Was Implemented at *All Saints, Pawleys*

After Chuck Murphy became the rector and senior pastor of *All Saints, Pawleys*, attendance and giving began to increase dramatically; and they continued to increase in spite of the controversy that was evolving simultaneously within The Episcopal Church. Even visitors who attended *All Saints, Pawleys* recognized immediately that this was not your typical "Episcopal" church. *All Saints, Pawleys'* twentieth rector and visionary priest, Chuck Murphy, was building a new paradigm church upon the foundations that had been laid by the matriarchs and patriarchs for almost three centuries.

Between 1982 and 2003, the average Episcopal congregation in the United States *lost* one-third of its members. Between 1982 and 2003, *All Saints, Pawleys* *gained* 688 new members. Between 1982 and 2003, average Sunday attendance at *All Saints, Pawleys* increased 422% from 163 to 851 as the graph below illustrates.

Average Sunday Attendance (ASA) at
All Saints, Pawleys
1982-2003

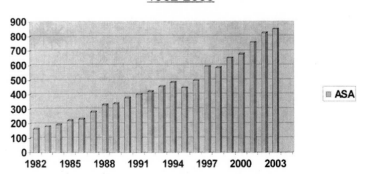

The Crisis of Faith and Leadership Within The Episcopal Church

In *The Gathering Storm*, sociologist Jeffrey Hadden described a storm that had hit the American mainline churches with a vengeance in the 1960's. According to Hadden, the churches in the United States (and in the United Kingdom) were presented with a threefold crisis: a crisis of meaning and purpose, a crisis of belief, and a crisis of authority.

In 1997, as the crisis of faith and leadership was evolving within The Episcopal Church, Chuck Murphy invited thirty theologically conservative Episcopal bishops, priests, and lay-leaders from around the country to a meeting at *All Saints, Pawleys* in order to discuss the crisis and to discern what if anything could be done to combat it. Murphy had not read *The Gathering Storm*, but since his ordination as an Episcopal priest, he had witnessed first-hand the growing crisis of faith and leadership that was developing within The Episcopal Church precisely as Hadden had predicted that it would, almost forty years earlier.

The First Promise Roundtable and the "AMiA"

The group of theologically conservative Episcopalian leaders that met at *All Saints, Pawleys* in 1997 established the *First Promise Roundtable* which led ultimately to the consecration in Singapore of Chuck Murphy and John Rodgers as "Missionary Bishops" *to* the United States. Soon thereafter, the *First Promise Movement* began, and then the *Anglican Mission in America* (the AMiA) which later morphed into the *Anglican Mission in the Americas* when the mission expanded into Canada. Today, the AMiA remains a "missionary outreach" of the Anglican Church of Rwanda, although, it is also a "ministry partner" with the theologically conservative

Anglican Church of North America (the ACNA) that v established in 2009.

According to Bishop Murphy, the purpose of the AMiA was two-fold: (1) to reach the approximately 130 million unchurched Americans with the Gospel of Jesus Christ, and (2) to offer an alternative to other orthodox Episcopal priests and congregations who felt that they could no longer remain within The Episcopal Church. Since its inception in 2000, the AMiA has planted an average of one new congregation every three weeks throughout the United States and Canada.

For decades, a group of ladies at *All Saints, Pawleys* had prayed regularly that God would send a godly, gifted, and anointed pastor to lead their congregation. So, for many, Chuck Murphy was the answer to their prayers. Chuck Murphy the man, was stellar in their eyes; but it was the first century worship and leadership model that the man taught and taught and taught that produced the real remarkable growth and transformation at *All Saints, Pawleys.*

Introduction to the First Century Worship
and Leadership Model

Since the general decline in membership and attendance within the mainline churches begin in the mid 1960s, sociologists of religion have attempted to identify "local institutional factors" that have contributed to the growth and decline of local congregations. The "local institutional factors" that contributed to the phenomenal growth at *All Saints, Pawleys* were embedded in the unique worship and leadership model that Chuck Murphy taught and implemented at *All Saints, Pawleys* during the 23 years that he served as its rector and senior pastor.

According to Murphy, the second chapter of Acts describes the eight building blocks of the early church. These eight building blocks are the essential components of what this book refers to as the first century worship and leadership model. Three years before Chuck Murphy left *All Saints, Pawleys*, he taught the eight building blocks of the early church for the last time during nine adult classes that were held following the Sunday morning worship services. On the first Sunday, Murphy introduced the series by describing his understanding of the role of the church in the world. According to Murphy:

> The church is God's idea. It is God's plan for this age. The things that we do are more than personal preference. They are a part of God's plan for us. The subject of the church lies at the very heart of the Bible. The Scriptures describe a movement of God that has gone from the old covenant, which emphasized the law and doing, to the new covenant, which emphasizes grace and being. The old covenant was embodied in a nation, Israel, while the new covenant is embodied in the church, the new Israel. The church is the body of Christ. The clergy contribute to the church by preaching and teaching the truth; but it is the body, the laity, that God encounters, equips, and launches to build His Church and His Kingdom.

For the next eight weeks, Chuck Murphy taught each of the eight building blocks of the early church. In 2010, Murphy was invited by Bishop David Pytches and several others to teach this first century worship and leadership model in the United Kingdom. Murphy was surprised by how receptive people were to this teaching that they had apparently never heard. A publisher who attended the teachings was so impressed that he offered to publish the texts of Murphy's messages.

The following chapters contain excerpts from these lectures, in Chuck Murphy's own words. Each of the excerpts is followed by a brief commentary by the author.

5

The Word is Proclaimed

Acts 2:14: *Then Peter stepped forward with the eleven other apostles and shouted to the crowd: Listen carefully all of you, fellow Jews and residents of Jerusalem!*

The first component of the first century worship and leadership model is the Proclamation of the Word. Chuck Murphy taught:

> On the day of Pentecost, Peter stood up and proclaimed the Word; and it was through this preaching that the church was birthed and built. Preaching allowed those in the early church to encounter God through his Word. The early church preached three things: a person, a gift (the Holy Spirit), and a need to respond; but the emphasis was always on the person, Jesus.
>
> The apostles proclaimed Jesus, the truth—an unapologetically supernatural Gospel, which transcended the natural world. This is what caused people to respond. At All Saints, Pawleys, this is preached because Jesus preached it. Jesus said: I am: the way, the truth, the door, the vine, and he

demonstrated it. Jesus was and is both the messenger and the message.

What is the Word, the Gospel, the Good News, that was proclaimed? The Word is not a thing. It is not rules and regulations. It is not an eight-fold path like Buddha advocated. The Gospel is a person, Jesus Christ. This is what is distinctive about Christianity. Jesus is the Good News. The Gospel is about a relationship with Jesus Christ. We are saved by Him, through a relationship with Him.

The sole purpose for All Saints, Pawleys is to introduce people to this person, to create an environment where people come to know him. At All Saints, Pawleys, Jesus is proclaimed, not social good, not some other theory or good intentions that may have some value to you or someone else. If churches do not preach Jesus, they are off the mark and will not flourish.

At All Saints, Pawleys, we preach not what we do, but what Jesus did. He is either going to be the foundation stone for everything that the church is building or the stumbling block which the church will trip over. You cannot avoid Him. Every knee will bow to Him in this world or the next.

Commentary

According to Murphy, Jesus changed the dominant theme in the Scriptures from "come and see" to "go and tell." Jesus commanded his disciples to go and preach the Gospel.

Preaching the Gospel of "Jesus, the Person" had been customary fare at most Southern Baptist and evangelical churches in the U.S. and the U.K. for over a century. However, this Gospel of "Jesus, the person" was not (and still is not) preached typically from the pulpits of the mainline churches in the United States or the established churches in the U.K. and Europe.

Proclaiming the Gospel of Jesus was something that Murphy and the other preachers at *All Saints, Pawleys* did well. One of Murphy's early assistants who possessed an exceptional preaching gift was Thaddeus Barnum. "Thad" Barnum and his wife Erilynne had trained for nine years under Terry Fullam at St. Paul's, Darien, prior to organizing a church in Pennsylvania, and subsequently moving to Pawleys Island. Barnum, who earned his Master of Divinity at Yale Divinity School, was regarded by many within the AMiA as one of the best expository preachers of our time.

The Expository Preaching of Thad Barnum Contributed Greatly to the Growth of *All Saints, Pawleys* During *The Murphy Years*

Thad Barnum modeled his preaching after that of Dr. Martyn Lloyd-Jones, a physician who later became an evangelical preacher at Westminster Chapel in London where he served as Vicar for thirty years. According to Dr. Jones: "Preaching is the highest and the greatest and the most glorious calling to which anyone can ever be called . . . . and as it is the greatest and the most urgent need in the Church, it is obviously the greatest need in the world also."[1]

Barnum insisted that scripture interprets scripture. Therefore, the Old Testament must be viewed through the lenses of Jesus Christ and the New Testament. His sermons also reflected the urgency that Martyn Lloyd-Jones spoke of, and he underscored the reality that there were two gates, two doors, and two paths: a narrow one and a wide one.

Two weeks prior to the consecration of Eugene Robinson as The Episcopal Church's first non-celibate gay bishop, Barnum preached that there were also two churches, those churches that received and believed "the faith once delivered to the saints," and those that had turned away from Scripture. He added that The Episcopal Church would be one of the latter if it consecrated Robinson. The next weekend, Eugene Robinson was consecrated as the Bishop of New Hampshire.

Few at *All Saints, Pawleys* would argue with the notion that Barnum's powerful proclamation of the Word contributed greatly to the growth in attendance that was experienced by *All Saints, Pawleys* during *The Murphy Years*.

Leaders from 69 Congregations Came to Visit
All Saints, Pawleys

Priests from around the country began to hear about the remarkable growth and transformation that was taking place at *All Saints, Pawleys*. Soon, many of them began to call, wanting to visit. Such visits were very time consuming for the staff. So, Chuck Murphy decided to bring in leaders from four congregations at a time for what were called "Visiting Vestry Weekends," and he decided to involve the *All Saints, Pawleys* lay leaders in the process. "This gave visiting vestries and lay leaders a chance to interact with our Vestry and lay leaders, and it gave me a chance to reinforce the vision with our own members," Murphy said. During the next ten years, priests and leaders from 69 Episcopal churches throughout the United States attended these Visiting Vestry Weekends at *All Saints, Pawleys*.

The Visiting Vestry Weekends were another step that *All Saints, Pawleys* took to live into its Vision Statement: "To become a people who risk boldly in sharing the Full Counsel of God, bringing encouragement *to the Church and to the World*" [emphasis added]. These Visiting Vestry Weekends brought encouragement to at least 69 other theologically conservative

Episcopal congregations that were located all over the United States.

Soon thereafter, *All Saints, Pawleys* would bring encouragement to still more orthodox Episcopal churches in the United States and Canada and to the worldwide Anglican Communion through the *First Promise Roundtable*, through Chuck Murphy's consecration in Singapore as a Missionary Bishop, and through the Anglican Mission in the Americas (AMiA).

Therefore, the proclamation of the Gospel of "Jesus, the person" by Chuck Murphy and the other preachers at *All Saints, Pawleys* attracted not only members by the hundreds, but also leaders from other churches around the country, and ultimately, from around the world. Thus, the proclamation of the Word must be considered the first *local institutional factor* that contributed to the phenomenal growth of *All Saints, Pawleys* during *The Murphy Years*, and the first component of the first century worship and leadership model, but there were others.

6

The Need is Acknowledged

The people needed what Peter was preaching and what God offered.

The second component of the first century worship and leadership model is the acknowledgement that people actually need the Good News that Peter was announcing. Chuck Murphy taught:

> There is a skeptical side of us that does not want to acknowledge the need for the Holy Spirit, but there is a believer side of us that is excited about the possibility of experiencing a movement of God that actually draws us to All Saints, Pawleys and empowers us for ministry. Without the Holy Spirit moving in a meaningful way, All Saints, Pawleys would not be the church that it was called to be. If All Saints, Pawleys wants to be an apostolic church, then it must have the same witness and power that the apostles had.
>
> All Saints, Pawleys must have apostolic faith so that it matters if someone wants to question or distort the faith. It also must be a church of apostolic witness which involves boldness and courage.

Everywhere the Apostles went, they created controversy. They were not chameleons that blended in with the cultural and social fabric of their day. The church is called to apostolic faith and apostolic witness; and the church is also called to apostolic experience.

The apostolic experience of the early church—what happened at Pentecost—made the disciples different. It was a new beginning, a new creation, the birth of the church. The apostolic experience equips us to make us effective. If we are uncomfortable with this, we are more like the churches that Paul was preaching to in Acts 19, before he laid hands on them for the anointing of the Holy Spirit.

The Old Testament Judges received power from the Spirit (Judges 3:10: The Spirit came upon him.) The Prophets received the Spirit (2 Kings 2:9: Let me inherit a double portion of your Spirit.) The Prophets promised the gift of the Spirit, and after a 350 year silence, John the Baptist came and said: I baptize you with water but [Jesus] will baptize you with the Holy Spirit and fire (Matthew 3:11). This is something that is available to average, normal people, but they must acknowledge the need for it.

The Holy Spirit is the key to everything that happens after the ascension: apostolic life and apostolic experience (the gifts and the fruits of the Holy Spirit). We are not Christians without it. Christian means anointed one. This is the experience that God wants for us. We pray: Come Holy Spirit; we ask for an encounter with the living God.

Terry Fullam of St. Paul's, Darien taught: We receive the Holy Spirit when we become Christians; however, we receive the anointing of the Holy Spirit later in order to begin new ministry. It is this anointing that enables us to be more effective in new ministries. We are leaking buckets; so, we need to receive the anointing of the Holy Spirit again and again in order refill our buckets so that we can enjoy the fruits of the Spirit. We need this gift, and that is why the Holy Spirit must be a part of the message of the local church.

If All Saints, Pawleys is proclaiming the Word, it is proclaiming what Jesus is and does and what the Holy Spirit is and does. The Holy Spirit points us to Jesus, and Jesus points us to the Father—it is an encounter with God.

Commentary

With this teaching about the "Holy Spirit," Chuck Murphy not only departed from the typical Sunday morning preaching and teaching offered in most mainline churches in the United States, he had also taken a step away from the teaching of many Southern Baptist and evangelical churches in the United States and the United Kingdom. While the evangelicals were comfortable with preaching "Jesus, the person," teaching and preaching about the "Holy Spirit" was an entirely different matter.

Yet, in the four congregational studies that were discussed previously, not just the "theologians", but also the "academicians"–the "social scientists"—acknowledged that those congregations that were growing had met the innate need that people have for transcendence—their desire to encounter the living God through the "Holy Spirit." In this second component of the first century worship and leadership model, Chuck Murphy unapologetically acknowledged the believers' need for the Holy Spirit, and he characterized that need as a window through which the work of the Holy Spirit could be examined and experienced.

Murphy stated not only that believers needed the anointing of the Holy Spirit, but also that they needed to receive this anointing again and again because we are all leaking buckets. Thus, we become dry and ineffective as apostolic witnesses from time to time. Therefore, Murphy created two distinct opportunities for members to receive this anointing of the Holy Spirit at *All Saints, Pawleys.*

<u>Chuck Murphy Created an Opportunity for Healing Prayer and the Anointing of the Holy Spirit During the Sunday Worship Services</u>

The first opportunity occurred during the regular Sunday worship services. "Prayer Teams" manned "prayer stations" in rooms behind the altar. The priests who celebrated holy communion invited those who came forward to receive the bread and the wine to go to "a place apart," in order to receive prayer for the anointing of the Holy Spirit.

Those who wanted prayer simply exited to the right and were escorted back to a private room where two to three prayer partners laid hands on them and prayed for any need that was expressed. Often, the members simply requested to receive the anointing of the Holy Spirit. Therefore, receiving prayer and the anointing of the Holy Spirit during Sunday worship was not a public event at *All Saints, Pawleys,* as it is typically in charismatic and Pentecostal churches.

The Toronto Airport Fellowship was an example of a church where the anointing of the Spirit was a public event. During the 1990s, people from all over the world traveled to Toronto to receive the anointing of the Spirit at this church. At the conclusion of the service, most of those in the congregation would move quickly to painted sets of footprints around the circumference of the auditorium. Once everyone was in place, prayer teams would move down the line of footprints laying hands on the people, praying for them, and catching those who fell to the floor, "resting" in the Spirit.[1]

People occasionally rested in the Spirit at *All Saints, Pawleys*; however, during Sunday worship, such occurrences always happened in a place apart from the main sanctuary. The gifts of the Spirit were not on display during the Sunday morning services at *All Saints, Pawleys*.

The Wednesday Services Provided Another Venue for Healing Prayer

Chuck Murphy created another venue for people to receive healing prayer and the anointing of the Holy Spirit at the "Healing Service" that was held every Wednesday morning across the street in the "Old Church," the smaller historic sanctuary. In this service that was typically attended by more mature believers, the gifts of the Spirit were displayed more openly. The prayer partners sometimes prayed in tongues (*glossolalia*), and many of those who came forward for prayer "rested" in the Spirit after receiving prayer for an anointing of the Spirit.

No place apart existed in the Old Church for people to go. Therefore, the gifts of the Spirit could be observed by all who attended this service. Murphy felt strongly that the ministry of the Spirit should be experienced by all of the members of *All Saints, Pawleys*.

Chuck Murphy taught that Jesus sent the disciples out to show the people the power of God by healing them and casting out demons. Murphy also observed that Americans live in an experience economy. They pay $5.00 for a cup of coffee at Starbucks when they could pay $1.00 for a cup at McDonald's. Why? For the experience. When people come to church, they want to do more than hear a good sermon and some uplifting music, they want to experience the living God; and if they do, they will return again and again.

Very few mainline churches in the United States or in the United Kingdom teach about the role of the Holy Spirit in the church because such teaching makes their members uncomfortable. Even fewer churches create an opportunity for their worshipers to *experience* the gifts of the Spirit. Therefore, visitors from other congregations attended *All Saints, Pawleys* often just to hear the teaching about the Holy Spirit. Some of those who visited became regular attendees so that they could learn more about and experience the power of the Spirit.

Therefore, the teaching about the Holy Spirit at *All Saints, Pawleys* and the creation of opportunities for people to receive the anointing of the Spirit and to experience the gifts of the Spirit were also very effective *local institutional factors* which contributed significantly to the unusual growth of *All Saints, Pawleys* and represent the second component of the first century worship and leadership model.

7

Baptism

Acts 2:37-38: *Peter's words pierced their hearts, and they said to him and the other apostles, "Brothers, what should we do?" Peter replied, "Each of you must repent of your sins and turn to God, and be baptized in the name of Jesus Christ for the forgiveness of your sins."*

The third component of the first century worship and leadership model was Baptism. Chuck Murphy taught:

> After Peter's sermon, people were cut to the heart. The need was acknowledged. People were empty. So, they asked: "What shall we do?" Peter responded: Repent and be baptized.
>
> All people have to make choices. As people respond to the power of the Holy Spirit, it is important for us to hold up the most important choice that people have to make—the choice of what kind of death they want. The choice of what type of death that a person wants is reflected in his Baptism. Baptism is going to make a difference in the life of the person.

We live in a world that says that Baptism does not really matter. The world is offended when we say that we are not all God's children, but that is precisely what the theology of Baptism teaches. We are all creatures of God, but we are not all children of God. We must be adopted as sons and daughters by Him through Baptism. We are all given the opportunity to become children of God, but we must respond. Baptism makes a difference that makes a difference.

The promise, the offer that God makes, is wrapped up in Baptism. Baptism is something that happens by God's grace, and it provides for our adoption as his sons and daughters. We are called into a relationship with Jesus Christ to be changed from one degree of glory to another—to be transformed—and this relationship starts with Baptism. Baptism is not just a preference; it has eternal significance.

What we are doing at All Saints, Pawleys is not just for religious types. What we are doing is essential and urgent. It matters. What we are trying to present to people is that choices are being made and that there will be a time when it is too late to make the right choice. We are all headed for death. We can choose our life, and we can choose our death. Baptism makes a difference that makes a difference.

Commentary

For Chuck Murphy, this component of the first century worship and leadership model, Baptism, was non-negotiable, an essential element of the early church and the church of the 21st century. According to sociologist Martin Stringer, Baptism for the New Testament writers was the sign of a change of life, the distinguishing feature of those who had received the Spirit.

However, by the beginning of the third century, Baptism had become a rite of entry into the church.[1] Thus, as the church began to define its boundaries in response to theological controversies, the experience of the individual became subordinate to the concerns of the institution.

In teaching this component of the model, Chuck Murphy stressed that Baptism was instituted as a sacrament by Jesus Christ. Murphy taught that all people are *creatures* of God. God created everything. However, all people are not *children* of God. The sacrament of Baptism was necessary in order to become a "child" of God, to attain "Sonship," and thus receive the promises of Scripture.

8

The Apostles' Teaching, Fellowship, and the Eucharist

Acts 2:42: *All the believers devoted themselves to the apostles' teaching, and to fellowship, and to sharing in meals (including the Lord's Supper), and to prayer.*

The fourth component of the first century worship and leadership model consisted of the apostles' teaching, fellowship, and the Eucharist. According to Murphy:

> The apostles' teaching is always the defining work of the church because faith comes through hearing the Word of God. The Word of God written shapes us. The church is under the authority of Scripture.
> Fellowship occurs when two or more people gather in His name. Fellowship is an opportunity for God to: (1) speak to His people through His people; (2) touch His people through His people; (3) encourage His people through His people; (4) heal His people through His people; (5) bless His people

through His people; and (6) correct His people through His people.

Finally, on the last night of his earthly life, Jesus gave us the Eucharist, or Holy Communion, which Catholics and Anglicans also refer to as a sacrament. A sacrament is not just religious action. A sacrament is a way in which non-physical reality is communicated through physical channels. William Temple, the Archbishop of Canterbury from 1942 through 1944, once said: "Christianity is the most materialistic religion in the world. God likes matter. He invented it."

The material world is where we live, and God uses it to communicate with us. Matter is not evil, nor is it an illusion as the Eastern religions claim. For five days, God created matter before he created man. Later, the Word became Flesh. This is the way God likes to work. We see it in the face and person of Jesus Christ.

What happened on the last night of Jesus' life at the Eucharist? He took, blessed, broke, and gave the bread of life to his disciples. This is the same thing that he did when he fed the four thousand and the five thousand. He established this rhythm that we need to continue. What really happens in the Eucharist is an actual encounter with God through a very physical channel. This is the rhythm that we maintain today in Sunday worship. We hear the story told. We rehearse the action: taking, blessing, breaking, giving. There is an encounter, an engagement, but before that, the Holy Spirit works. Otherwise, it would be just religious action.

What we ask is for the Spirit to descend upon us and the bread and wine. The Holy Spirit makes the elements and us holy. We are sanctified, and thus we connect with God. It is not the only way to connect with God, but it is a real way to encounter God. Anglican Churches have big pulpits and big altars—

the proclamation of the Word and the celebration of the Eucharist matter. The Word is proclaimed; the need for the Holy Spirit is acknowledged. Then, we enter into a relationship with God through Baptism, and we are sustained in that relationship through the Eucharist.

Commentary

Three *local institutional factors* and components of the first century worship and leadership model can be identified in this fourth building block of the early church: the apostles' teaching, the fellowship of the believers, and the Eucharist. With respect to the Apostles' Teaching, one of the first things that Chuck Murphy did when he arrived at *All Saints, Pawleys* was to begin teaching the "Adult Study" that later became known as the "Adult Forum." Unlike the adult Sunday school classes at most congregations, Chuck Murphy, the senior pastor, taught the adult class at *All Saints, Pawleys*.

THE APOSTLES' TEACHING
The Adult Class

When he first became Rector at *All Saints, Pawleys*, Murphy had no Assistant Rector or Curate. Therefore, he had to prepare several teachings each week: the sermons for the Sunday and Wednesday services, plus the teaching for the Adult Class. However, Murphy was committed to all of these because he felt that worship should include the proclamation of the Word, the celebration of the Eucharist, and the Apostles' Teaching.

Murphy was a very effective teacher; therefore, people were drawn to his Adult Study. According to A. H."Doc" Lachicotte, the patriarch of the congregation, "Within one year after Chuck Murphy started teaching the Adult Study, there were more people attending the

Adult Class than had been attending the two Sunday worship services combined a year earlier."

All Saints, Pawleys Became a Teaching Center with "Jan Term at Pawleys"

Murphy also brought in outside speakers to preach and teach at *All Saints, Pawleys*, and one of his dreams was to establish a teaching center on the campus that would give the *All Saints, Pawleys* members, and others from around the country, the opportunity to hear the best and the brightest Christian teachers in the world. *All Saints, Pawleys* took the first step toward becoming such a center, when it began hosting *Jan Term at Pawleys*, a month-long cooperative teaching venture with Trinity School for Ministry in Pittsburgh, Pennsylvania.

At these "Jan Terms," seminary students from Trinity Seminary were given the opportunity to study and experience life at one of The Episcopal Church's largest and most vibrant congregations, and the *All Saints, Pawleys'* members were given the opportunity to hear some of the best teachers and preachers in the worldwide Anglican Communion.

The Institute for Christian Leadership

Chuck Murphy took the next step toward making *All Saints, Pawleys* a teaching center by establishing the *Institute for Christian Leadership* on the campus of *All Saints, Pawleys*. The Rt. Rev. Alex Dickson, Bishop of West Tennessee, moved to Pawleys Island following his retirement, and Chuck Murphy asked him to become the "Bishop in Residence at All Saints, Pawleys" and to serve as the "Interim Dean" of the Institute for Christian Leadership.

Less than one year later, Dr. Philip W. Comfort, an internationally recognized New Testament scholar and the New Testament editor for both the NIV and the NLT Bible translations, moved to Pawleys Island after his wife had been miraculously healed from inflammatory breast cancer. Georgia Comfort's cancer was gone, but her physician told here that her immune system had been suppressed by the high doses of chemotherapy that she had received. He suggested that she and Phil consider moving to a place with warmer winters.

The Comforts visited Charleston, South Carolina, and then ventured north to Pawleys Island. According to Philip Comfort:

> I just walked into All Saints, Pawleys one day and asked Chuck Murphy if he had ever considered starting a seminary. I told him that I had two degrees, one in Greek and another in New Testament Studies. Immediately, Chuck Murphy named me "Dean" of the Institute of Christian Leadership.

Comfort taught Greek and New Testament book studies at the Institute, where students also studied homiletics (preaching) under Thad Barnum, and congregational development and leadership under Chuck Murphy and Tim Surratt, the pastor of the contemporary service at *All Saints, Pawleys*. The students at the *Institute* received credit for courses taken toward a Master of Divinity from Trinity School for Ministry in Pittsburgh, Pennsylvania, and later, from Columbia Biblical Seminary in Columbia, South Carolina.

FELLOWSHIP
The second element of this component of the the first century worship and leadership model was *fel-*

lowship. For Chuck Murphy, fellowship involved much more than a group of believers gathering for a covered-dish dinner. For Murphy, fellowship meant believers gathering in small groups to pray, to study God's Word, and to expect God to move, touch, speak, and guide them.

Murphy attended a workshop presented by Carl George on the *Meta-Church* paradigm. According to George, the *Meta-Church* paradigm consisted of a local congregation that was committed to joyous corporate worship (celebration) and to the formation of nurture groups and ministry teams (cells) that were led by lay pastors. Multiplication of these *cells,* according to George, allowed unlimited numerical expansion, without sacrificing quality.[1]

Cell Churches and the Acts 2:42 Groups at
All Saints, Pawleys

In his book, *Cell Church Solutions,* Dr. Joel Comiskey documented the explosive growth of "cell churches" internationally. Comiskey observed that many of the largest Christian churches were cell churches, including Yoido Full Gospel Church in Seoul, Korea, the largest church in the world.[2]

After Murphy's return from the *Meta-Church* workshop, *All Saints, Pawleys* launched what it called *Acts 2:42 Groups.* These groups met weekly, outside of the church, typically in homes, but Chuck Murphy set the agenda for the meeting. Each group consisted of a "lay leader" and an "observer" who would replace the leader when the group divided and multiplied.

Chuck Murphy personally taught monthly training sessions for the lay leaders and observers of the groups, who then facilitated weekly meetings in their homes. These lay leaders then invited people to join their Acts 2:42 Groups, and the leaders were encouraged to include non-members of *All Saints, Pawleys.* As a result, some members in the community experienced a home Bible study for the first time, and many of them soon began attending *All Saints, Pawleys.*

Therefore, these Acts 2:42 Groups were another local institutional factor that contributed to the growth of *All Saints, Pawleys* during *The Murphy Years* and are an essential component of the first century worship and leadership model.

Chuck Murphy's Consensus Model of Leadership

Sociologists of religion Dean Hoge and David Roozen determined that "member involvement" was another factor that was highly correlated with church growth. The Acts 2:42 Groups were one example of member involvement. Another example was reflected in Murphy's "consensus model of leadership." One of Murphy's mantras that he repeated often was: "God speaks to his people through his people." Murphy not only taught this concept. He lived it through his leadership style.

The "Vision" Was "Presented" at Vestry Retreats

The canon law of The Episcopal Church delegated the management of the temporal affairs of the congregation (the money and the property) to the elected lay leaders, who are called the "Vestry." In addition to the monthly business meetings of the Vestry, however, Murphy scheduled at least one, and sometimes several, "Vestry Retreats" each year. These two day retreats were held away from the *All Saints, Pawleys* campus. At these retreats, Chuck Murphy would share what he sensed was God's vision for *All Saints, Pawleys* "for its next season"—its "preferred-future."

The members of the Vestry would hear the vision presented, pray for discernment, and then break into small groups so that God could speak to his people through his people. Then, the Vestry members would reconvene, and representatives from each small group would report back to Murphy telling him if the group had reached a consensus about any of the topics that had been presented. Murphy would record each group's responses on newsprint.

The "Vision" Was "Confirmed" by Leaders at an Annual Leadership Conference

Those parts of the vision that seemed pleasing to the Vestry members and to the Holy Spirit were then presented to a larger group of leaders from the congregation at an "Annual Leadership Conference" that was held typically in November of each year. These leadership conferences resembled the early "church councils" where godly people gathered in order to let God speak to his people through his people. Thus Murphy's consensus model of leadership was consistent with the "conciliar tradition" of the early church.

The leadership conferences were attended by over one hundred present and former Vestry members, present and former Wardens, and other invited lay leaders of the congregation. At these leadership conferences, Chuck Murphy would present the vision again that had now been clarified, and perhaps narrowed or altered at the preceding Vestry Retreats. This presentation would again be followed by prayer for discernment and discussion in small groups. Following the discussion, one member of each group would report back to Murphy any consensus that had been reached by his or her group.

The "Vision" Was "Adopted" at the Annual Parish Meeting

Any items upon which a consensus was reached at the Leadership Conference, and only those items, would be presented to the full membership for their approval at the annual congregational meeting in January. Therefore, prior to the meeting in January, those presently serving on the Vestry and over one hundred members had reached a consensus on the vision and preferred future of *All Saints, Pawleys*.

This consensus leadership style emphasized prayer and discernment on the part of the laity which Murphy considered *fellowship*. Allowing the laity to participate in the vision-casting at these Vestry Retreats and Leadership Conferences enabled *All Saints, Pawleys* to embrace many bold projects, like building a new and larger sanctuary and a multi-million dollar teaching center, and ultimately, withdrawing from The Episcopal Church.

All Saints, Pawleys Voted to Withdraw from The Episcopal Church in 2004

At a specially called meeting held in January 2004, 468 of the 507 members of *All Saints, Pawleys* voted to sever all ties with The Episcopal Church. God had spoken to his people through his people. Few congregations could match the harmony and the unanimity that this first century worship and leadership model produced at *All Saints, Pawleys* during *The Murphy Years*.

THE EUCHARIST

Finally, Chuck Murphy also maintained that the "Eucharist" (referred to as Holy Communion in the 1662 English *Prayer Book* and in the 1928 American *Prayer*

Book) was a critical element in the first century worship and leadership model. Most Episcopal congregations use the liturgy for *Morning Prayer* for Sunday morning services. The Eucharist is celebrated typically once each month, or at most, every third Sunday. Such had been the case at *All Saints, Pawleys* prior to the arrival of Chuck Murphy. Murphy insisted that the Eucharist be celebrated *every* Sunday (and Wednesday).

The practical effect of celebrating the Eucharist every Sunday was to lengthen the Sunday worship service from 60 minutes to at least 90 minutes and sometimes longer depending on attendance. This 90 minutes did not include an additional 45 minutes for the Adult Class that many of the members also chose to attend. However, many of the members that transferred their memberships to *All Saints, Pawleys* had attended non-liturgical churches, so the Eucharist provided an element of holiness and contributed to the awe, wonder, and transcendence that these newcomers were seeking.

Pawleys Island is a retirement community where the beach, the river, the golf courses, and other Sunday afternoon diversions abound. Thus, one would have expected the attendance at *All Saints, Pawleys* to have decreased in response to the lengthened worship services. To the contrary, the average attendance at Sunday worship services increased significantly after the Eucharist began to be celebrated every Sunday.

According to Murphy, one of the attractions of classical Anglicanism is that it combines the proclamation of the Word with the power of the Holy Spirit and the sacraments of Baptism *and* the Eucharist. Attendance increased consecutively for twelve years after Murphy began celebrating the Eucharist every Sunday.

Therefore, the apostles' teaching, the fellowship as expressed in the Acts 2:42 Groups and Chuck Murphy's consensus leadership model, and the weekly *Eucharist* were all *local institutional factors* that contributed greatly to the growth of *All Saints, Pawleys* during *The Murphy Years*, and were also essential components of the first century worship and leadership model.

9

Miracles, Awe, and Power

Acts 2:43: *A deep sense of awe came over them all, and the apostles performed many miraculous signs and wonders.*

The fifth component of the first century worship and leadership model included a teaching about the miracles, awe, and power that those in the early church experienced. Chuck Murphy taught:

> Wonder and awe are needed in the church today. We don't need more religion. We need more contact with the living God. What we need to understand is that what had been promised by the prophets hundreds of years before Christ became real to the apostles at Pentecost, and it is available to us today.
>
> There is a global movement of God in the world today that has been happening before our very eyes for over one hundred years [the Pentecostal movement]. What has happened in this last century is phenomenal. Of the two billion Christians in the world today, 27 percent call themselves Pentecostal, over 500 million people.

God is doing something global. By 2025, forty-four percent of the Christians in the world will call themselves Pentecostal. The promise of the prophets, John the Baptist, and Jesus is still unfolding today. Also, the fact that two-thirds of these Pentecostals are located in the two-thirds world (the Southern Hemisphere sometimes referred to as the Global South) is forcing a restructuring of the whole Christian community. A whole new culture is being created. Catholicism used to be the global common denominator; soon it will be Pentecostalism.

Thirty years ago while I was studying at Trinity College in Bristol, England, I asked Malcolm Widdecombe, the Rector of Pip 'n' Jay, to lay hands on me and to pray for me to be anointed by the Holy Spirit. I had an amazing encounter that was initially both exciting and scary. Later, I experienced a level of boldness that I had not enjoyed in the past. God gave me a boldness to say: "Let's go for it!" This boldness has held me through a lot of storms. Ministry is not for sissies. Ministers need wisdom, discernment, an anointing to preach, and the power of the Holy Spirit to see the vision that God has for his people.

Soon after my arrival at *All Saints, Pawleys*, the congregation began to open up to this power of the Spirit. *All Saints, Pawleys* said: "Let's go for it!" It spent money it didn't have. It built big buildings it did not yet fully need. *All Saints, Pawleys* did things that people said you don't have to do to be a serious Episcopal church. The boldness unfolded. It was a move of the Spirit. *All Saints, Pawleys* began to make a difference that made a difference, and people began to notice the awe and wonder. They were drawn to it.

An excellent example of this awe and wonder was "Women in Discipleship," a discipleship program that had begun as an Acts 2:42 Group around Erilynne Barnum's dining room table. The Holy Spirit anointed Erilynne Barnum, and the program grew locally to include over 600 ladies from 30 different churches. By 2006, Women In Discipleship had evolved into the Call to Discipleship program that had been adopted nationally by over 150 churches and internationally by churches in seven countries including Holy Trinity, Brompton in London, the home of "The Alpha Course."

"Women" had to be dropped from the name because soon men began embracing the program as well. Erilynne was a gifted teacher, but it was the anointing from the Holy Spirit, the power, that people began to notice and were drawn to.

The bottom line is that the power of the Holy Spirit is available today, and that is good news.

Commentary

While *miracles* did occur at *All Saints, Pawleys*, in his teaching on this component of the first century worship and leadership model, Chuck Murphy chose to stress the concept of "awe and wonder"—the power, the presence, and the movement of God within the local congregation. According to Murphy, Jesus sent the disciples out two by two to "show" people the Gospel. He gave them very little content. He wanted them to show people the Gospel by healing the sick and driving out demons—with *signs and wonders.*

In his book, *Pentecostal Anglicans,* John Gunstone described how the Pentecostal movement began to sweep through the Church of England in the mid 1960s. According to Gunstone, many Church of England parishes found their worship and life being shaped by this renewal, including Pip 'n' Jay, Bristol and St. Thomas' Crookes, Sheffield.[1] The pastors of both of these Church of England parishes played a prominent role in the life and growth of *All Saints, Pawleys* during *The Murphy Years.*

The Influence of Pip 'n' Jay, Bristol and St. Thomas' Crookes, Sheffield

Chuck and Margaret Murphy were assigned to Pip 'n' Jay as their "home church," while Murphy studied at Trinity College, Bristol. Later, Murphy discovered that the faculty at Trinity College had intentionally sent him to Pip 'n' Jay so that he could experience the movement of the Spirit that was occurring there. Many at *All Saints, Pawleys* felt that Murphy had brought the "anointing" that he received at Pip 'n' Jay back to Pawleys Island, especially those who attended the Wednesday healing services.

Also, the Rev. Mike Breen, the Team Rector of St. Thomas' Crookes, Sheffield, was a regular visitor to *All Saints, Pawleys* during *The Murphy Years* where his preaching and teaching skills always drew large crowds. St. Thomas' Crookes, Sheffield grew to become one of the largest Protestant churches in Europe after Breen became Team Rector there in 1994.[2] In, 2009, Mike Breen and his entire coaching team at 3D Ministries, moved to Pawleys Island; and Breen and his partner, Steve Cockram, began preaching and teaching regularly at *All Saints, Pawleys.*

The Wednesday Healing Services Attracted Many Visitors

Just as Chuck Murphy had insisted that the Sunday worship services contain the proclamation of the Word, the Eucharist, and the Apostles' Teaching, he insisted that the Wednesday morning healing services contain the proclamation of the Word, the Eucharist, and the "Ministry of the Holy Spirit." Word spread quickly about the Wednesday services, and the number of visitors at these services often exceeded the number of members from *All Saints, Pawleys*. Often, ministers and members of other congregations would attend the Wednesday services. These visitors came for the teaching and anointing of the Holy Spirit because it was not taught and offered at their home churches.

At the Wednesday morning healing services, the prayer-time would begin at approximately 11 o'clock immediately following the celebration of the Eucharist. On some occasions, these healing services lasted for several hours. The length of the services depended upon the number of people who came forward for healing prayer. The service was referred to as the "healing service" because many people came forward asking for prayer for physical and emotional healing, in addition to asking for the anointing of the Holy Spirit.

Physical Healing Occurred Occasionally
at the Wednesday Healing Services
Mrs. Pat Moody, from Georgetown, South Carolina, was one of those, who came forward for healing prayer during the Wednesday service. Pat Moody and her husband, Doug, lived in Georgetown where they were active members of the First Presbyterian Church. In late 1995, the Moodys sold their home and made plans to retire in Florida. However, one night prior to the move, Doug Moody awoke to find Pat unconscious in a pool of blood.

Pat was rushed to Roper Medical Center in Charleston, South Carolina, where she was diagnosed with colorectal cancer. Dr. Julian Buxton, a prominent surgeon in Charleston, told the couple that Pat had an inoperable, malignant tumor the size of a grapefruit. Buxton added that the cancer had metastasized into

Pat's liver and lungs, and he estimated that she had no more than three weeks to live.

Pat Moody worked at a gift shop in the *Hammock Shops*, a village of retail shops in the center of Pawleys Island, and one of Pat's co-workers told her about the Wednesday morning healing services at *All Saints, Pawleys*. Pat attended one of these services and described her experience this way:

> A lady named Martha Brown met me on the front steps of the church and insisted that I sit up front, so that I could be the first to receive prayer. When the members of the prayer team began to pray for me, I felt waves of light washing over me. I had never experienced anything like that, but I realized that I had been healed, right then.

The next day, the Moodys traveled to Roper Hospital in Charleston for a CT scan that had been previously scheduled. Pat Moody's radiologist and her surgeon soon confirmed what she had already sensed—the cancerous tumor was gone. Dr. Buxton is now deceased; however, his associate, Dr. Jonathan Donaldson, confirmed the extent of Pat Moody's disease in a letter to the author dated January 23, 2006:

> Patricia Moody has been under my care since June of 1996. She was diagnosed with invasive, metastatic, non-operable, squamous cell cancer of the anal canal in 1996. Since then, there has been no sign of cancer recurrence.

In early 2011, the Moodys were still worshiping at *All Saints, Pawleys*. According to Pat Moody, they cancelled their plans to retire in Florida because she refused to live anywhere that would prevent her from worshiping the living God at *All Saints, Pawleys* every Sunday and every Wednesday.

Pat Moody's experience was not unique. At each Wednesday morning healing service, Chuck Murphy would ask for praise reports from anyone who felt that the prayers offered on their behalf had been answered. One such report came from Bud Willis, a successful textile executive, who lived in nearby Litchfield Beach.

A Textile Executive Was Healed at the
Wednesday Morning Service

Bud Willis had been forced into retirement from his job at Cone Mills, a textile conglomerate, when he was diagnosed with a rare and terminal type of leukemia. After being turned down for a bone marrow transplant at Seattle Pacific University Hospital, Willis attended the Wednesday morning healing service. Willis described his experience this way:

> As soon as I went forward for prayer, I experienced something that I had never experienced before. It is difficult to describe, but when they began praying for me, it was as if a bright light was shining on me. I felt warm all over. I knew at that moment, instantaneously, that my life had changed, that I was going to survive.

Soon thereafter, much to his doctor's surprise, Willis' leukemia went into permanent remission, and he was able to return to full-time employment. Willis, who at that time attended a Southern Baptist church, and in 2011 was attending a United Methodist church, added: "I have never been to a church service like that. I know that I am alive today because of the healing prayer that I received at the Wednesday healing service at *All Saints, Pawleys*."

Ironically, neither Pat Moody nor Bud Willis were members of *All Saints, Pawleys* when they attended their Wednesday service. Members of *All Saints, Pawleys* had heard about their plights and invited them to come to the Wednesday healing service. As Ed Stetzer would say: "Many of the members of *All Saints, Pawleys* were engaged in the meaningful ministry and mission of God." They were not "passive spectators."

Some Who Were Prayed For at the Wednesday Services Were Not Healed

Many who came to the Wednesday healing services were healed. The author's wife was healed from inflammatory breast cancer (the same cancer that had inflicted Georgia Comfort), but some who received prayer at these services were not healed.

In 2001, Howard Early, a successful entrepreneur from Louisville, Kentucky, was diagnosed with inoperable kidney cancer. When chemotherapy failed to shrink his tumors, he traveled 685 miles to *All Saints, Pawleys* in order to attend the Wednesday healing service.

When Early returned home, his doctors found that his tumors had shrunk considerably. Early did not survive, but he credited the healing prayer that he received at *All Saints, Pawleys* with prolonging his life, giving him several additional months of quality time with his family.

Even Local Physicians Came to the Wednesday Services for Healing Prayer

Dr. Robert Speir, a radiologist and devout Roman Catholic from nearby Myrtle Beach, heard about the

Wednesday healing services, and he came to the Wednesday service for healing prayer from a terminal illness. Speir was accompanied by his family and by two of his fellow physicians at Grand Strand Regional Medical Center: Dr. Neil Trask, the chief of cardiology, and Dr. Ed Shelley, the chief of radiology.

Dr. Speir was not healed, but the fact that these three prominent Myrtle Beach physicians and their families, none of whom were Episcopalians or attended *All Saints, Pawleys*, came to the Wednesday healing service, expecting to encounter the Holy Spirit and believing that the power of the Spirit could heal Dr. Speir, spoke volumes about the ministry and mission that was taking place at *All Saints, Pawleys* during *The Murphy Years*.

<u>Chuck Murphy Says That The Fact that All</u>
<u>Were Not Healed is a Mystery</u>

From time to time, the members of *All Saints, Pawleys* would ask Chuck Murphy why some were miraculously healed and others were not. Murphy would reply: "It is a mystery that God has not revealed to us yet," adding that he had recently watched both his father and his younger sister die of cancer after they had both received much healing prayer.

In his book, *The Mind of Jesus*, William Barclay made this observation about miracles and healing prayer:

> The fact is that [the apostles] lived in an age which expected miracles. There is a kind of rationalism that kills wonder. When wonder is dead, wonderful things cease to happen. We might well receive more miracles, if we stopped insisting that miracles do not happen, and began expecting them to happen.[3]

Many at *All Saints, Pawleys* expected miracles to happen, and they witnessed many of them.

Therefore, the *miracles, awe, and power* experienced by the members at *All Saints, Pawleys* through the prayer ministry and the ministry of the Holy Spirit at the Wednesday healing services must also be considered *local institutional factors* that contributed greatly to the growth of *All Saints, Pawleys* during *The Murphy Years* and were essential components of the first century worship and leadership model. At *All Saints, Pawleys*, the members and visitors did not just hear theologically conservative teaching and preaching, they also *experienced* the living God and *expected* miracles to occur through the power of the Spirit.

10

Stewardship

Acts 2:44-45: *And all the believers met together in one place and shared everything they had. They sold their property and possessions and shared the money with those in need.*

The sixth component of the first century worship and leadership model was stewardship. Chuck Murphy taught:

> Stewardship is the most troubling component of the model for most people. People can get comfortable with the other components, even the gifts of the Spirit; but they remain uncomfortable with the concept of stewardship. Stewardship is investing in God's agenda. Stewardship is what one does after he says he believes.
> In Jesus' teaching, stewardship mattered. One-third of the parables of Jesus dealt with stewardship, and one-sixth of his recorded words dealt with stewardship. Therefore, if we want to be a people of God, we must get comfortable with this component. Jesus thinks it matters. He said: "Where your treasure is,

there will your heart be also." Look at your check-book, and you will see where your heart is.

It is true that stewardship is about more than money, but money matters. Money is muscle that the church needs. When I went into the ministry, I told God that I was going to give him all of my time and my talents, but God said: What about your money? Even clergy have to deal with the money thing.

The concept of the tithe is unique because it is not taught with respect to time and talent; it is only taught with respect to our treasure. Acts 2:44-45 does not refer to the tithe. The early church invested in God's agenda in a profound way—they sold every-thing and gave to anyone who needed it. The tithe is just ten percent, a fraction of what we saw in the early church; and we even have trouble with that. In God's eyes, it is his money. God thinks that we are stewards of his money, not the owners of it.

When I came to *All Saints, Pawleys*, the largest pledge was $7,500; twenty years later it was $75,000. What happened? Money is muscle. If you invest in God's agenda, you are investing muscle in God's agenda. There is a principle here that is important to God: the sacraments. Sacraments are physical channels for expressing non-physical realities. God communicates with us through physical channels, and this same principle works in reverse. One of the ways that we communicate with God is with our money. Money is a physical channel for expressing our sacrificial giving. Money matters to God.

Commentary

Chuck Murphy had taught the biblical basis of stew-ardship at Episcopal churches around the country for several years before he came to *All Saints, Pawleys*, and he also taught it repeatedly, and effectively, during his tenure at *All Saints, Pawleys*. When Murphy arrived at *All Saints, Pawleys*, the total giving by its members, through pledges and offerings (known in Episcopal circles as "Plate and Pledge"), was $131,384, and the average giving per member was $287. Twenty years later, the total giving had increased to $1,764,123, and the average giving per member had increased to $2,610.[1]

Giving at *All Saints, Pawleys* Was Four Times the National Average

According to the *Yearbook of American & Canadian Churches,* the average giving per member for American congregations was $627.[2] Therefore, the average giving per member at *All Saints, Pawleys* was over four times greater than the national average. Giving at All Saints was also over four times greater than the giving at the average Episcopal congregation in the Diocese of South Carolina where the average giving was $612, slightly below the national average.

According to parochial data published by the Diocese, *All Saints, Pawleys* ranked number two in total giving out of all 75 churches in the Diocese, and *All Saints, Pawleys* ranked number one in giving per member. These rankings were remarkable when one considered that the population and affluence of Pawleys Island paled in comparison to other areas of the Diocese (e.g. Charleston, Kiawah Island, and Hilton Head Island) that had much larger Episcopal churches many of which were filled with wealthy retirees.

Members Were Encouraged to "Strive Toward the Tithe" and to Give to Capital Projects

Chuck Murphy encouraged the members at *All Saints, Pawleys* to strive toward the tithe, but he also encouraged them to give sacrificially to capital funds, so that *All Saints, Pawleys* could build newer and larger buildings on its campus. Murphy was a proponent of the "eighty percent rule" which maintains that growth in attendance stops when attendance reaches eighty percent of the capacity of the meeting space. Bill Hybels, Pastor of *Willow Creek Church* in Chicago says that having "maximum available seats at peak worship times" has contributed to the record growth at Willow Creek.

Chuck Murphy stated frequently: "Visitors will not return, if they have difficulty finding a seat." As a result, during Murphy's tenure, the members at *All Saints, Pawleys* gave approximately $6 million over and above their tithes to construct four new buildings on the campus to accommodate the steady stream of new members and visitors.

The Research Findings of a Study on Giving

The giving at *All Saints, Pawleys* was even more remarkable when one considered the findings of a study of 625 American congregations in five different denominations that was conducted by sociologists of religion Mark Chaves and Sharon Miller. In *Financing American Religion,* Chaves and Miller observed: The highest givers to [American] churches tend to be between forty and sixty years of age, were married, and had children at home.[2] Pawleys Island is a retirement community. Therefore, most of the large givers at *All Saints, Pawleys* were over sixty-five years of age, and very few of the members had young children at home.

After its launch, the "Access" contemporary service at *All Saints, Pawleys* began to attract young married couples with children at home. However, most of those who attended Access were not big givers, and the majority of them were under forty. Therefore, *All Saints, Pawleys* did not conform to the typical parameters discovered by Chaves and Miller. The implementation of the first century worship and leadership model had transformed *All Saints, Pawleys* into a new paradigm church.

The Institutional Embeddedness of Giving

Chaves and Miller also examined the differences in giving by denominations. They concluded that Presbyterians and Roman Catholics typically gave because of a concern for "institutional survival," as a result of what Chaves and Miller described as the "institutional embeddedness of giving."[3] Chaves and Miller did not study Episcopalians; however, two other sociologists of religion analyzed NORC *General Social Surveys* and concluded that Episcopalians gave an average of 1.5 percent of their incomes to their churches, compared to Catholics who gave an average of 1.25 percent, and Presbyterians who gave an average of 2.5 percent. Therefore, one could argue that the institutional embeddedness of giving also exists within the typical Episcopal congregation in the United States.

According to Chaves and Miller, "If people believe that the reason they should give is to maintain the services of the church, then they give enough to do that and little more. [However] if giving is seen as part of a larger scheme—representative of one's relationship with God, or meeting the needs of others, more is given."[4]

Chuck Murphy Taught the Theology of Stewardship

During *The Murphy Years* at *All Saints, Pawleys*, Chuck Murphy did more than preach stewardship sermons. Murphy taught the "theology of stewardship," and this teaching helped the members of *All Saints, Pawleys* focus on their personal response to the Gospel message: the *missional needs of the church*, rather than the *institutional needs of the congregation*. Murphy addressed the question of what stewardship has to do with the good news of the Gospel, what it means, and why it is important.

At *All Saints, Pawleys*, the theology of stewardship was taught; the pledges were tabulated; and then the budget was established by the Vestry based on the total amount pledged. Thus, the *missional needs* of the church were funded by the amount pledged. The budget was not determined by the *institutional needs* of the congregation.

Chuck Murphy's stewardship teaching at *All Saints, Pawleys* was extremely effective. Therefore, this teaching should be considered yet another *local institutional factor* that contributed greatly to the growth of *All Saints, Pawleys* during *The Murphy Years* and a critical component of the first century worship and leadership model.

11

Worship

Acts 2:46-47: *They worshiped at the Temple every day, met in homes for the Lord's Supper, and shared their meals with great joy and generosity—all the while praising God and enjoying the goodwill of all the people.*

The seventh component of the first century worship and leadership model was worship. Chuck Murphy taught:

> If you blow Sunday morning, you have blown it. On Sunday morning, something happens when God's people gather. We must work on it. We must give it our best shot in the preaching, the teaching, the music, and the like. Most of the 331,000 congregations in the United States do not have very good attendance. Half of them cannot gather 75 people, including children, on Sunday morning.
>
> Seventy-five percent of all congregations do not have 140 people gather together for Sunday services. Eighty-five percent cannot break the 200 average Sunday attendance barrier. You must structure things differently to break the 200 attendance barrier. You must teach, teach, and teach. Ninety

percent of congregations cannot break the 400 hundred attendance barrier that All Saints, Pawleys broke in 1991. Finally, less than one percent of congregations break the 800 attendance barrier that All Saints, Pawleys broke in 2002.

Thus, one of the important components of the first century model is what happens in Sunday worship. The world is crying out for an encounter with God—a real and actual meeting with God. If you show me a place where God is showing up—where God is moving—I will show you a place where people are showing up on Sunday. If the apostles' teaching takes place, signs and wonders are seen, and serious stewardship takes place, people will say: "I'd like to check that out." People want to meet with God, and if they do on Sunday morning, then they will come back.

For this to happen, for genuine worship to occur, someone must explain worship and actively teach it. That is why at All Saints, Pawleys we offered Thursday night teachings on "instructed prayer and praise" and "national worship conferences," so that we could teach people how to worship. We didn't just let it happen; go with the flow, like most churches did. Genuine worship requires us to be intentional—to learn how to worship. God has been teaching us how to worship from the very beginning.

Look at Genesis, Chapter 4. Cain and Abel brought sacrifices to the Lord. God told Cain: That is nice, but Abel's sacrifice is closer to what true worship will involve (blood poured out, rather than fruit offered up). We have to learn how to worship. Consider the woman at the well. Jesus said: "You worship you know not what; but the hour is coming when you will worship in Spirit and in Truth."

The Holy Spirit points us to the truth of the Gospel being taught, to the Eucharist, to the signs and wonders. The Holy Spirit convicts us. Sometimes it stings. It may not be a feel-good bubbly thing, but it is a step into deeper worship. The Spirit fills us. We are the temple of the Holy Spirit, and that infilling is important according to Paul.

Some people use the Oran position. They lift their hands in worship. This was not an invention of the charismatics—it is the oldest known worship position. It signifies that you are open to receive anything that God is offering through the Spirit. On Sunday at All Saints, Pawleys, we say: "Come Holy Spirit, come."

The prophetic happens on Sunday. God speaks to his people through his people—through the teaching, through the Eucharist, through the prayers, through the Spirit—as much today as He did in the first century. We ask for wisdom: "Fill me with the knowledge of your will." We must be open to the possibility that God may want to give us the gift of tongues [glossolalia] because we don't know how to pray as we ought (Romans 8:26). Paul prayed in the Spirit. If you don't want it, no one will give it to you; but, it is important to ask for it, to expect it.

We ask for healing. When you go back for prayer during the Eucharist, you should expect God to show up, for things to happen. We cannot make God do things, but we can ask and expect God to show up in real ways.

We are to worship in Spirit and truth. God needs to reveal to us what his truth is. He does this through worship: through preaching, through teaching, and through the Spirit. He fully intends to change you from one degree of glory into another through the Spirit (2 Corinthians 3:18). Nothing you can buy, or do, or accomplish can do this for you but the Savior. We need the Savior who came to seek and save the lost. So, we come into Sunday worship. We have something to be thankful for, to offer praise for. This generates an attitude of gratitude that spills over into worship.

All of this requires revelation. You find it throughout the Scriptures. In Genesis, God taught Abraham how to worship "Bring me a heifer" (Genesis 15:9). He also taught Jacob how to worship, and Jacob acknowledged: "Surely the presence of the Lord is in this place" (Genesis 28:16). Worship must be guided by God, directed by God. It comes out of a revelation.

We are not creative enough to do worship without God's revelation. We have to have God himself show us how to worship. The disciples said: "We don't know how to pray." So, Jesus taught them the Lord's Prayer. When we come to church with our skewed attitudes, we need to pause a minute and say: "I need to step into the presence of God, into this moment." It requires God's revelation in the face of Jesus, but it also requires our action.

Sixty-six out of seventy-two times, the Greek word for worship that was used in the New Testament was *proskuneo* which means to fall before the Lord, to kiss his feet or the hem of his garment. It required a decision. God wants us to come close to Him, to fall before Him. That takes our action. We have to come to the table with something. God does his part, but we have to do our part.

The preacher preaches the sermon, and the laity pray the prayers of the people; but someone else must also provide the music. Music really does matter; it shapes our worship. We have to constantly work on it. St. Augustine said: "He who sings prays twice." We may be in a grumpy mood at first, but when we hear the music, we start tapping our toes. We don't even know why. Music matters. In the scriptures, genuine leaders in worship were always involved with music. David danced before the Lord. Solomon had the temple orchestra. We must keep working on it. We must ask the Lord to take all of this and help us to worship because we don't know how to worship on our own. The apostle Paul said to make melody with all of your hearts.

Leith Anderson has said that when people go to a restaurant, they expect to find food. When people go to the theatre, they expect to see a movie. When people go to church, they expect to meet God. What we are about here at All Saints, Pawleys is creating a space and a place where people can meet God. People are crying out for this encounter. Music helps that kind of thing happen because when we step out of ourselves and into the worship, we encounter God.

Rick Warren said that worship is a place and a moment in which the purposes for our lives and the world are revealed: where God's pardon is to be offered, where His presence is to be felt, and where His power is displayed. We want to step into an environment where the power of the Lord is moving. We sing during communion: "The power of the Lord is moving in this place." It is a gift and a grace that is needed. This is what worship is about at All Saints, Pawleys.

Commentary

This seventh component of the first century worship and leadership model, *worship*, was a critical factor that contributed to the transformation and growth of *All Saints, Pawleys* during *The Murphy Years*. From his first day at *All Saints, Pawleys*, Chuck Murphy maintained: "If you blow Sunday worship, you have blown it." Therefore, Murphy's approach was one of *intentionality* toward worship, especially Sunday worship.

The Sunday Services Didn't Just Happen at *All Saints, Pawleys*

Sunday worship did not simply happen at *All Saints, Pawleys*. Chuck Murphy choreographed it. According to Murphy, "It takes intentionality on our part and the power of the Holy Spirit to get the people's toes tapping. If you lose them, you have lost them for the rest of the service." Thus, Murphy made certain that the worship flowed, deliberately and continuously, until its conclusion.

Donald Miller observed a similar phenomenon during the worship services at Calvary Chapel churches. According to Miller, no one was asked to recite a creed, read the Scripture, or even listen to the morning announcements—nothing was allowed to break the mood.[1] Murphy did not want to break the mood either. He wanted to keep the toes tapping. However, he was able to accomplish this feat *and* have the people recite the Nicene Creed, read the Scripture, and listen to announcements. Murphy was able to create a space and a place within the traditional Anglican liturgy for the Spirit to move—for people to encounter the living God.

The Introduction of Praise Music into the Blended Service

One of the most significant contributions that Chuck Murphy made to the Sunday worship at *All Saints, Pawleys* was the introduction of contemporary praise music into what became known as the *blended service*. This service blended contemporary praise music into the traditional Anglican liturgy, along with music from The Episcopal Church Hymnal. Some members at *All Saints, Pawleys* who had attended *Cursillo* renewal weekends and worship conferences needed no introduction to praise music, but very few of the members (and even fewer of the visitors) had been exposed to praise music when Murphy introduced them to it.

Murphy would ask those who worshiped at *All Saints, Pawleys* to enter fully into the worship because God inhabits the praises of his people. Murphy also stressed the intimacy of worship, as he urged those at *All Saints, Pawleys* "to draw near to kiss" the living God, by singing the praise songs and entering fully into the worship.

Donald Miller described the music in new paradigm churches as a form of sacred lovemaking, transcending the routinized rituals that so often structure human-divine communication.[2] Daniel Albrecht offered a similar description of Pentecostal and charismatic worship services:

> In a very real sense, the services are designed to provide a context for a mystical encounter, an experience with the divine. This encounter is mediated by the sense of immediate divine presence. The primary rites of worship and praise are particularly structured to sensitize the congregants to the presence of the divine and to stimulate a conscious experience of God.[3]

All Saints, Pawleys was not a Pentecostal church, but Chuck Murphy would agree with both Miller and Albrecht. He could point to the tears that streamed from the eyes of the members and visitors during Sunday worship as evidence of the presence of the divine when they sang:

> Surely the presence of the Lord is in this place,
> I can feel your mighty power and your grace.

I can hear the brush of angel's wings, I see glory on
    each face;
Surely the presence of the Lord is in this place.
And
Open our eyes Lord, we want to see Jesus,
Reach out and touch him and say that we love Him,
Open our ears Lord, and help us to listen,
Open our eyes Lord, we want to see Jesus.
And
O Lord, you are beautiful,
Your face is all I seek,
And when our eyes are on this child
Your grace abounds; your touch is all I need.
And
I love you Lord, and I lift my voice,
To worship you, O my soul rejoice,
Take Joy my King in what you hear,
Let me be a sweet sweet sound in your ear.
And
Spirit of the Living God, fall afresh on me.
Spirit of the Living God, fall afresh on me.
Melt me, mold me, fill me, use me.
Spirit of the Living God, fall afresh on me.

In typical Pentecostal church services in the
United Kingdom and in Calvary Chapel and Vineyard
Fellowship churches in the United States, a series of
praise songs, like these, were sung at the beginning of
the worship. This is sometimes called "block-worship".
The music was used to block out whatever baggage that
the people brought with them to church. At *All Saints,
Pawleys*, these praise songs were sung throughout the
service and continuously during communion.

Not every one sang these songs, but even those
who did not sing experienced something that they had
not experienced before—the awe and wonder of an

encounter with the living God—something that occurred when the Spirit fell afresh on the congregation.

Unlike, the typical Pentecostal worship services, no one spoke in tongues during the Sunday services at *All Saints, Pawleys*, although prophecies were occasionally shared. However, the Spirit showed up during the Eucharist as the members sang the praise music. So many people shed tears that boxes of tissues had to be placed in the pews.

The Services from the *Prayerbook* and the *Hymnal* Were Combined Into *The Parish Family Worship Book*

In the early days of *The Murphy Years*, All Saints, Pawleys had "Guest Sundays" to which the members were urged to bring their friends and neighbors. Most of the visitors at these Guest Sundays were not Episcopalians, and they often had difficulty juggling the *Prayer Book*, the *Hymnal*, and the *Bible*. Therefore, Murphy produced a *Parish Family Worship Book* that combined the liturgy and the praise songs into one book.

Years later, the music at All Saints became more sophisticated, and the tissue boxes gradually began to disappear from the pews. However, those members who had been attracted initially by the worshipful, praise music were now both engaged and challenged by the preaching and teaching of Chuck Murphy, Thad Barnum, David Bryan, and the outside teachers and preachers that Murphy brought to preach and teach at *All Saints, Pawleys*.

The Composition of the Congregation

When Chuck Murphy arrived at *All Saints, Pawleys*, the composition of the congregation was not unlike that of the typical Episcopal congregation. *All Saints, Pawleys* typified the *graying of America*. A survey of the membership twenty years later revealed that 76 percent of those who attended the 8 a.m. traditional service at *All Saints, Pawleys* were over age 65, and 44 percent of them were over age 75.

When Chuck Murphy came to *All Saints, Pawleys*, the age distribution of the 10 a.m. service was similar to that of the 8 a.m. service twenty years later. However, after Murphy introduced praise music into the 10 a.m. service, so many young couples with children were attracted to *All Saints, Pawleys* that the entire children's ministry program had to be revamped and bolstered.

Therefore, by introducing the contemporary praise music into the 10 a.m. service, Murphy had successfully blended the needs and the desires of the retirees and the young couples with children to encounter the living God through worship. The chart below shows the age distribution of those who were attending the 8 a.m. traditional service and the 10 a.m. blended service during *The Murphy Years*.

Age Distribution of the Traditional and Blended Services at *All Saints, Pawleys*

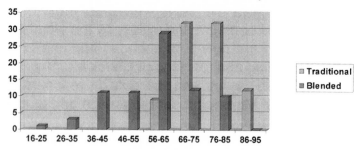

Source: 2005 *All Saints, Pawleys'* Membership Survey

The sixty and seventy-year-old members were still in abundance at *All Saints, Pawleys* after the introduction of the blended service. However, the new service also attracted a considerable number of thirty, forty, and fifty year olds. According to the membership survey, these younger members were attracted to *All Saints, Pawleys* by the preaching, the music, and the fellowship in that order.

The Access Contemporary Service

Another significant innovation in worship that Chuck Murphy introduced at *All Saints, Pawleys* was contemporary worship. Chuck Murphy attended a conference at Willow Creek Community Church in Chicago; and when he returned, he informed the members of the Vestry that the largest group of unchurched people in the world no longer lived in Africa, Asia, or Latin America. Rather, the largest group of unchurched people in the world consisted of the "twenty-somethings" that lived in the United States.

According to research done by Willow Creek, most Americans stopped attending church during their late teens or early twenties, and few of them returned to church during their twenties. If a twenty-something were bold enough to attend an American church service, he or she would realize quickly that there were few, if any, other people in their twenties attending the service; so, in all probability, he or she would not return.

Therefore, Murphy decided that *All Saints, Pawleys* must launch a service for twenty-somethings. Some of the members of the Vestry were skeptical. One member said that that she could count the number of twenty-somethings in Pawleys Island on one hand, and she knew because her daughter was one of them. Despite this skepticism, the contemporary service was launched in the "Parish Hall", a more informal space than the sanctuary.

The skeptics were correct, at least initially. The new service struggled to attract 25 people, and most of those who attended were not twenty-somethings. Nevertheless, Murphy soon asked the Vestry to fund a full-time staff person to lead the contemporary service. The Vestry agreed, and Murphy called Tim Surratt, whom Murphy had worked with at Trinity Cathedral in Columbia, South Carolina. When Murphy called him, Surratt was serving as the youth minister at St. Philip's Episcopal Church in Charleston, South Carolina.

Tim Surratt, a Former Youth Pastor, Became the Senior Pastor of "Access"

According to Surratt, his years in youth ministry, and many short-term mission trips with teenagers to Haiti, had taught him how to attract young people to church and how to get them involved. Surratt quickly began using these skills to attract the "twenty-somethings," the "thirty-somethings," the "forty-somethings," and some even "older and wiser" people to "Access," the contemporary service at *All Saints, Pawleys*. According to the *All Saints, Pawleys'* Membership Survey, 65 percent of those who attended the contemporary service were age 45, or younger.

Composition of Access Contemporary Service

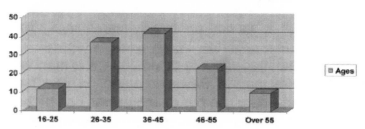

Surratt, and his largely volunteer staff, encouraged people to dress casually, grab a cup of coffee, and come on in to experience the living God. The venue was different, but the message was the same, and *All Saints, Pawleys* had successfully reached the twenty and thirty-year-olds that the traditional and blended services (and most other Episcopal congregations in the United States), had been unable to attract. Access adopted the following purpose statement: to create an environment where we come to know and worship Jesus Christ through relevant messages, fine arts, and music.

According to the *All Saints, Pawleys'* Membership Survey, the preaching, the fellowship, and the music were the primary reasons that new people were attracted to Access. Craig and Jackie Beaumont, professional musicians at the *2001 VIP* nightclub in nearby Myrtle Beach, were drawn to *All Saints, Pawleys* and became the core of the Access Praise Band. Surratt also incorporated drama into the service.

Under Surratt's leadership, average Sunday attendance at Access grew from 123 to 300 in less than five years. Then, Chuck Murphy's eighty percent rule kicked in. The Access service had moved from the Parish Hall to the new ACTS Building (the Adult Center for Teaching and Study) when the new building had been completed; however, even the ACTS Building could not accommodate the growing congregation, especially during the summer months.

So, Surratt and the leadership at Access moved Access off of the *All Saints, Pawleys'* campus and re-named it "Grace Church" in an effort to reach even more unchurched people in the Pawleys Island area. Soon thereafter, Terrell Glenn, Chuck Murphy's successor at *All Saints, Pawleys*, implemented a new contemporary worship service at *All Saints, Pawleys*; and within two years, average Sunday attendance at the new contemporary service exceeded the attendance of the 8 a.m. traditional service and the 10:30 a.m. blended service combined.

Nine in the Morning—Failing Forward

One may get the impression that every innovation in worship that Chuck Murphy attempted at *All Saints, Pawleys* was successful. Most were, but the last worship service that Chuck Murphy launched at *All Saints, Pawleys* was not. Two years before his retirement, Murphy and a worship team launched a new service called *Nine in the Morning*.

This service took its name from Dennis Bennett's book, *Nine O'Clock in the Morning*. In the book, Bennett, an Episcopal priest, described his experience of being *baptized in the Spirit* while he served as the rector and senior pastor of an Episcopal church in Van Nuys, California.

According to Chuck Murphy, the *Nine in the Morning* service was an attempt to cast a *different net* in order to catch *different fish* that were not being caught by the other three services. Most of the Nine in the Morning service was projected onto a retractable screen, and the music was contemporary; but the priests still wore their vestments, and the large, formal, sanctuary did not lend itself to this type of informal worship.

After attending a Nine in the Morning service for the first time, Chase McGill, a twenty-something attorney from nearby Georgetown described his experience this way: "The sermon was good, and I liked the music; but all the robes and stuff gave me the creeps." This first time visitor to Nine in the Morning soon found a church home at the Access contemporary service (no vestments were worn during the Access services), as did some others who had attended the Nine in the Morning service.

After a one year trial, Chuck Murphy announced humbly from the pulpit that the Nine in the Morning service would be discontinued. Instead, a combined blended service would begin at 9:30 a.m., which would be followed by an Adult Forum at 11:30 a.m. each Sunday.

The combined attendance of the Nine in the Morning service and the eleven o'clock blended service had peaked at 386; however, according to Murphy, the additional 61 people that the Nine in the Morning service had added did not justify the disruption that had occurred in the congregational life by splitting the 10 o'clock service into two services. Much to his surprise, Murphy received a standing ovation from the congregation when he announced the cancellation of the Nine in the Morning service.

According to leadership expert, John Maxwell, one of the traits of a leader is his willingness to risk, and then to admit it, when something goes wrong. Maxwell describes this as *failing forward*.[4] Chuck Murphy did not fail often, but when he did, he *failed forward*; and he had done so by canceling the Nine in the Morning service.

A Pentecostal Worship Experience

In the 1980s, many pastors in the United Kingdom and in the United States had attempted to introduce elements of the Pentecostal experience into their Sunday worship services, but most were unsuccessful. Chuck Murphy was successful in doing so for two reasons. First, he introduced praise music and certain elements of Pentecostal worship gradually *into* the traditional liturgy, rather than jettisoning the liturgy completely as many American and English churches had done. Like his mentor, Malcolm Widdecombe at Pip 'n' Jay, Bristol, Murphy was able to create a space and a place for people to experience God within the traditional Anglican liturgy.

Professors Philip Jenkins, Harvey Cox, and Donald Miller and the Pew Forum on Religion and Public Life have researched and written extensively about the evangelical, Pentecostal, and charismatic churches that are exploding in number around the globe, especially within the Global South (Latin America, Africa, and Southeast Asia). Jenkins was the keynote speaker at an AMiA Winter Conference that was held at *All Saints, Pawleys.*

In his speech to over 1,000 North American Anglicans, Jenkins stated that evangelical, Pentecostal churches in the Global South were presenting themselves as modern-day bearers of an apostolic message that is not limited by geography, race, or culture. According to Jenkins, "Claims of signs and wonders serve as these churches' credentials."[5] Jenkins could just as well have been describing the miracles, awe, and wonder that the members of *All Saints, Pawleys* experienced each week when they encountered the living God during worship on Sundays and Wednesdays.

Harvard professor Harvey Cox has observed that churches that introduce Pentecostal elements into their worship services grow because Pentecostalism involves the experience and the expression of the primacy of religion and spirituality, not unlike its expression in the first century church (and in typical worship services at *All Saints, Pawleys.*)[6]

The Pew Forum on Religion and Public Life also has published an in-depth study of Pentecostalism.

The Pew study described Pentecostalism and related charismatic movements as one of the fastest-growing segments of global Christianity. According to Pew, at least one fourth of the world's 2 billion Christians are thought to be members of these lively, fast-growing congregations.

All Saints, Pawleys Was Not a Pentecostal Church During *The Murphy Years*

All Saints, Pawleys was not and is not a Pentecostal congregation. However, Chuck Murphy recognized that Americans live in an *experience economy*. Therefore, he sought to blend the best of the Pentecostal experience into the worship services at *All Saints, Pawleys*, just as he had blended the contemporary praise music into its worship services.

The results speak for themselves. Over 800 people from 10 different denominations (less than two percent of whom were Pentecostals) were attracted to *All Saints, Pawleys* because they were able to experience the living God through this worship model without having to deal with what Roger Olson and others have referred to as the "dark side of the Pentecostal movement."

In his last sermon at *All Saints, Pawleys*, the Rt. Rev. Alex Dickson, Bishop in Residence, declared: "It has taken me eighty years, but I can now say that I am an evangelical, charismatic, catholic, Anglican disciple of Jesus Christ." Hundreds in the congregation applauded in apparent agreement.

People from all over the country began coming to *All Saints, Pawleys* to experience the worship and to learn how to worship in Spirit and in Truth. Many Episcopalians began to refer to *All Saints, Pawleys* as "the little church that thinks that it is a cathedral." *All*

Saints, Pawleys had become a *new paradigm church*, and its intentionality with respect to worship was one of the *local institutional factors* that contributed significantly to its phenomenal growth during *The Murphy Years*.

12

Growth

Acts 2:47: *And each day the Lord added to their fellowship those who were being saved.*

The eighth and last component of the first century worship and leadership model is "growth". Chuck Murphy taught:

> In 2002, Christianity was growing faster than it ever had. Recently, Newsweek magazine had done a cover story and devoted eight pages to the explosive growth of Christianity worldwide. Since World War II, however, the United States, as a nation, had stepped back from religion and had removed it from the public sphere. Yet, in Africa, there were 1,200 new churches being started each month. They cannot build church buildings fast enough in Africa, Latin America, and Southeast Asia.
>
> Most churches in the United States just shuffle sheep among one another (a concept known in church growth circles as "sheep-stealing"). As a result, the United States has the largest unchurched English speaking population in the world, [147 million people]. Growth is so rare that people have

begun to wonder if God really wants it; or, people tend to de-emphasize it by saying that quality not quantity is what God wants.

They contend that God just wants us to love one another. The same is true in England. Supposedly, there are 24 million Anglicans in the United Kingdom, but less than 800,000, or 3 percent, presently attend church.

In the early church worship and leadership model, growth was not the first component, it was the last one. The first component was the proclamation of the Word. First, the Word was proclaimed, then people were cut to the heart. They felt the need to respond and were baptized. There were signs and wonders, and the people began to invest heavily in God's agenda. They also began worshiping in Spirit and Truth. Then, and only then, did growth begin to occur.

Growth was not the goal of the early church worship and leadership model. It was a by-product that resulted from all of the other components. The Lord added to their number daily after all of the other components were in place. Therefore, if a church uses the components that I have described [and implements the first century worship and leadership model described in this book], it can expect growth.

Growth can manifest itself in different ways. Twenty years ago when the population of Pawleys Island was less than 5,000 people, and it had one traffic light, I began to sense an inner growth at All Saints, Pawleys. God was rebuilding the foundation that was needed. We were growing up, discovering together the things that God wanted to show us.

We went to all kinds of conferences. We had the best and brightest speakers from around the world come in to tell us what God was doing and could do at All Saints, Pawleys. We knew that the Holy Spirit needed to be released in this place, so we created opportunities for that to happen.

You cannot make the Spirit move, but you can create opportunities for it to move. Cursillo renewal weekends were one of those opportunities. I served on two Cursillo teams during my first six months at All Saints, Pawleys.

We became more intentional about worship. We taught people how to worship, then attendance began to grow slowly. We broke the 200 average attendance barrier; I will never forget it. Eighty-five percent of congregations in America never break the 200 average Sunday attendance barrier. It was a big deal, and I was very grateful to God.

The old Parish Hall only seated 240, so we built a new and larger sanctuary in 1996 that seated 400. Some people in Pawleys Island (and at All Saints, Pawleys) asked incredulously: What is that new building, a monument to Chuck Murphy's ego?

At first, the new sanctuary felt huge because we were used to standing room only in the parish hall. We had to rope off the balcony and the back eight pews to feel any sense of community in the worship, but then God began to move. One thing that you have to realize is that when you reach 80 percent capacity, visitors will stop coming. The new sanctuary gave us the opportunity for new growth. The same thing happened at the Access service five years later when we built the ACTS Building in 2000.

Therefore, growth can be expected when all of the other components of the model are in place. The average Sunday attendance at All Saints, Pawleys in 2002 was over 800. This was greater than ninety-nine percent of the churches in the country. Why grow any more? The answer is because the Lord wants us to keep on reaching out, to keep throwing out nets. I believe that the Lord wants to continue to add to our number daily.

Therefore, growth is a by-product of a certain environment that we read about in the second chapter of Acts. There are certain things that a church can do to build a foundation for that growth. Even a 250 year old church like All Saints, Pawleys can create different opportunities for people to worship in. Here at All Saints, Pawleys, we have the Traditional (Rite I) Service, the Blended Service, the Access Contemporary Service, and the Wednesday healing service.

People can choose the service that they want to attend. Each service is an environment, a net designed to catch a certain type of person, which is effective as long as the Word is proclaimed and the Spirit is allowed to move. The trappings do not matter. The Lord said: "I want you to be fishers of men," and fishermen use different types of nets to catch different types of fish. That is why we have four different types of worship services.

Growth is something that is to be expected. It is something that we wait on, watch for, enjoy; something that I think God wants for All Saints, Pawleys. God purposes to build his church to draw those who do not yet know Him. At All Saints, Pawleys, we broke the 200, 400, 600, and 800 average Sunday attendance barriers. That is the vision that God had for All Saints, Pawleys, and that is the vision that I asked our members to embrace.

Commentary

After researching 1,000 churches in 32 countries on 6 continents, church growth expert Christian Schwarz concluded: "Increased worship attendance is not the ultimate goal with everything else being a means to an end; it is a natural by-product of improved quality."[1] Pastor Rick Warren of Saddleback Community Church in California agrees. Warren told over 4,200 Episcopalians who had gathered in Pittsburgh for the

Hope and a Future Conference: "All living things grow. Growth is a sign of health. The church is a body—an organism, not an organization. It must grow to survive." Chuck Murphy agreed with both Schwarz and Warren, and he cited the second chapter of Acts as his authority.

During *The Murphy Years, All Saints, Pawleys* Experienced Growth During 20 out of 23 Years and Double-Digit Growth During 7 of the 23 Years

In *The Churching of America,* Roger Finke and Rodney Stark asserted: "The most striking trend in the history of religion in America is growth."[2] One could make the same statement about *All Saints, Pawleys* during *The Murphy Years. All Saints, Pawleys* experienced growth in 20 out of 23 of *The Murphy Years*, and it experienced *double-digit growth* during 7 out of 23 of *The Murphy Years.* (See chart on next page)

Dwight Smith, a missiologist and the President of Saturation Church Planting International (SCPI), has studied the growth rates of Christian churches around the world. Smith, Jim Montgomery, and Donald McGavran were pioneers in the church growth movement in the Philippines during the 1970s. According to Smith, healthy churches normally experience an annual rate of growth of approximately two percent, which is considered biological growth, because it results from additional children being born to parents who are already members of the congregation.

Rates of Growth and Defining Moments at *All Saints, Pawleys* During *The Murphy Years*

	ASA	Change	Growth	Defining Moments
1982	163	n/a	n/a	Murphy began teaching the model
1983	181	18	11.04%	Eucharist celebrated every week
1984	194	7	3.86%	Contemporary music is introduced
1985	223	29	14.94%	ASP broke the 200 attendance barrier
1986	233	10	4.48%	The Rev. Rick Conrad became Assistant Rector
1987	281	48	20.60%	Youth ministry launched
1988	328	47	16.72%	MacNutt healing prayer conference
1989	339	9	2.74%	Acts 2:42 Groups launched
1990	377	38	11.21%	Visiting Vestry Weekends began
1991	403	2	6.89%	ASP broke the 400 attendance barrier
1992	421	18	4.46%	The Rev. John Barr becomes Co-Rector
1993	455	34	8.07%	*Jan Terms* begin with Trinity Seminary
1994	483	28	6.15%	National Worship Conferences begin
1995	447	- 36	- 7.45%	Institute for Christian Leadership established
1996	496	22	4.92%	Rev. T.J. Johnston becomes Assistant Rector
1997	593	46	9.27%	First Promise Roundtable convened
1998	585	- 8	- 1.34%	*Access* contemporary worship service launched
1999	652	67	11.45%	ASP broke the 600 attendance barrier
2000	677	25	3.83%	Chuck Murphy's consecration in Singapore
2001	757	80	11.82%	Rev. Thad Barnum named Interim Rector
2002	824	67	8.96%	ASP broke the 800 attendance barrier
2003	851	64	8.13%	Bishop Salmon vacates the Vestry
2004	804	- 47	- 5.53%	*All Saints, Pawleys* leaves TEC
2005	754	- 5	- 6.22%	Chuck Murphy retires as Rector of ASP

Source: All Saints, Pawleys, Annual Reports: 1982-2005; ASA is average Sunday attendance

Thus, according to Smith, consistent year to year growth of greater than two percent implies that something other than biological growth is taking place. The rate of growth at *All Saints, Pawleys* exceeded two percent in 19 out of 23 of *The Murphy Years* at *All Saints, Pawleys*.

Which Services at *All Saints, Pawleys* Attracted the Most People?

There are two aspects of the growth in Sunday attendance at *All Saints, Pawleys* that deserve further comment. For the first fifteen of *The Murphy Years*, there were only two Sunday morning worship services at *All Saints, Pawleys*: the 8:00 a.m. traditional service and the 10:00 a.m. blended service. One year after Chuck Murphy arrived, average attendance had increased at the traditional service to 74, and at the blended service to 142.

Fifteen years later, average attendance at the traditional service was 86, and average attendance at the blended service was 309. Therefore, most of the growth in Sunday attendance occurred in the blended service. These data support the notion that those who attended the blended service experienced the living God and the awe and wonder of the Spirit through the praise music and the prayer teams that were offered only in the blended service because the preachers and the preaching were identical in both services.

When *All Saints, Pawleys* launched its Access contemporary worship service, this service began to attract many young couples with small children. The table on the next page shows the average Sunday attendance for all three adult services plus the children's services for a five year period.

Average Sunday Attendance at
***All Saints, Pawleys'* Services**
1997 through 2002

	1997	1998	1999	2000	2001	2002	Growth
Traditional	86	87	85	74	73	64	- 22
Blended	309	283	331	300	305	343	+ 34
Contemporary	123	130	141	203	274	302	+ 179
Children	75	85	95	100	105	115	+ 40
Total	593	585	652	677	757	824	+ 231
Source: All Saints, Pawleys, *Annual Report: 2004.*							

Average attendance at Access almost tripled (from 123 to 302) during its first five years. Also, these data for Access did not include the growth of "Young Saints" and "Wee Saints," the children's ministries which also grew from 75 to 115. Nor did these data include the 125 middle school students who worshiped on Thursday nights or the 150 junior and senior high students who worshiped on Monday nights. Many of these students did not attend any of the Sunday services. Nevertheless, the rapid growth in Access also peaked when it reached 80 percent of the seating capacity of its venue, the ACTS Building.

The Sources of the Growth at *All Saints,*
Pawleys During *The Murphy Years*

A visitor to the blended service at *All Saints, Pawleys* once remarked to an usher: "This can't be an Episcopal church. There aren't this many Episcopalians in the whole state of Florida." There were not that many Episcopalians in Pawleys Island either. The *All Saints, Pawleys* membership survey revealed that over 60 percent of the members of *All Saints, Pawleys* were not Episcopalians when they first began attending *All Saints, Pawleys.*

Therefore, one aspect of the growth at *All Saints, Pawleys* that must be further examined is the source of its growth. Did the growth result from successful efforts by *All Saints, Pawleys* to reach the lost, the unchurched, or was it transfer growth ("sheep-stealing") from other area churches? Transfer growth results when members of other congregations in the same locality transfer their membership to a church like *All Saints, Pawleys* because of its superior preaching, music, or programs.

Was the Growth the Result of "Sheep-Stealing?"

The *All Saints, Pawleys'* membership survey revealed that only 23.5 percent of the members at *All Saints, Pawleys* grew up in the Episcopal church, and only 39.6 percent of the members had attended Episcopal churches prior to attending *All Saints, Pawleys.* Also, less than two percent of those who attended *All Saints, Pawleys* had been unchurched prior to joining *All Saints, Pawleys.* Such statistics imply that some "sheep-stealing" may have occurred at *All Saints, Pawleys.*

However, two *local contextual factors* argued against *sheep-stealing* on the part of *All Saints, Pawleys.* First, attendance increased also at the other four Protestant churches in Pawleys Island during *The Murphy Years.* Therefore, large numbers of members did not transfer from the other churches to *All Saints, Pawleys. All Saints, Pawleys* was able to attract a greater percentage of the newcomers to the Pawleys Island area than the other area churches.

When people transferred their membership into *All Saints, Pawleys,* they did so typically from churches in other cities, not from other churches in Pawleys

Island. According to the survey, the largest percentage of newcomers in Pawleys Island that joined *All Saints, Pawleys* were attracted to the "meaningful worship" that they experienced at *All Saints, Pawleys*. Meaningful worship was one of the *local institutional factors* that Hoge and Roozen identified as a major contributor to congregational growth.

Why did average Sunday attendance decline during four of *The Murphy Years*?

The second aspect of growth in attendance at *All Saints, Pawleys* that must be examined is the four years during *The Murphy Years* in which the average Sunday attendance *decreased*.

In 1992, the Rev. John Barr joined Murphy as "Co-Rector" of *All Saints, Pawleys*. Both Murphy and Barr acknowledged that no precedent existed in the Scriptures, or in the history of the Episcopal Church, for Co-Rectors. However, they agreed to implement this unique leadership model. Barr had served as the rector of *Christ Church* in Mobile, Alabama, and he brought both preaching and pastoral gifts to *All Saints, Pawleys*.

The "Co-Rector Model" Was Flawed and John Barr Left After Four Years

Murphy was a "rancher," not a "shepherd." He equipped others to provide pastoral care (visit the sick, elderly, etc.), but he rarely provided this pastoral care himself. Barr was more of a "shepherd," and the level of pastoral care that he provided was appreciated by many at *All Saints, Pawleys*. As a leadership model, however, the co-rectorship was flawed from the beginning, and Barr left *All Saints, Pawleys* in 1995. Many at *All Saints, Pawleys* were disappointed by Barr's departure, and at least 36 of them left the congregation when John Barr did.

The Crisis of Faith in The Episcopal Church Began to Take Its Toll

In 1998, average Sunday attendance decreased from 593 to 585. While the net decrease of eight members represented only one percent of the average Sunday attendance, this decrease was symptomatic of a larger disease. By the late 1990s, the liberal, revisionist bishops within The Episcopal Church were in control of the denomination, and the adverse implications of this fact had begun to trickle down into the local congregations, especially into theologically conservative ones like *All Saints, Pawleys*.

In 1998, a group of theologically conservative Episcopal priests and laypersons gathered for the second time at *All Saints, Pawleys*. At this meeting, the *First Promise Roundtable* issued a formal statement that urged the liberal revisionist bishops "to restore the faith delivered to the saints to The Episcopal Church." Murphy kept the *All Saints, Pawleys* members abreast of all of these developments, and most of them were fully supportive of his efforts. Some were not. In 1998, eight of them decided to worship elsewhere.

In 2004, Gene Robinson Had Been Recently Consecrated and *All Saints, Pawleys* Voted to Leave The Episcopal Church

In 2004, six years after that second meeting of the *First Promise Roundtable*, average Sunday attendance at *All Saints, Pawleys* decreased by 47 members, over 6 percent. Several possible explanations existed for this decrease in attendance including negative reactions to The Episcopal Church's consecration of Eugene Robinson as its first non-celibate gay bishop. However, another explanation was even more straightforward.

In January 2004, 468 members of *All Saints, Pawleys* voted to withdraw from The Episcopal Church. 38 others voted to remain in The Episcopal Church. Those 38 loyal Episcopalians, plus nine others, chose to worship initially in a nearby private school gymnasium before obtaining their own church building in Pawleys Island.

Until 2010, these 47 loyal Episcopalians, and others who had joined them, continued to hold themselves out at as the authentic *All Saints Parish, Waccamaw*. However, when the Supreme Court of South Carolina ruled that The Episcopal Church had no interest in the *All Saints, Pawleys* property, including its name, these loyal Episcopalians changed the name of their congregation to *Christ the King, Waccamaw Episcopal Church*.

While *Christ the King, Waccamaw* was not considered a "daughter church" by many in the *All Saints, Pawleys'* congregation, the author and some of the members at *All Saints, Pawleys* viewed *Christ the King, Waccamaw* positively as a successful church plant that was launched during *The Murphy Years*.

In 2005, *Christ Church, Murrells Inlet* Was Planted

Finally, in 2005, average Sunday attendance decreased by another 45 members. Of these 45 members, 39 transferred their memberships to *Christ Church, Murrells Inlet*, a new daughter church that *All Saints, Pawleys* helped establish in September 2005.

Therefore, the causes or sources of the *decreases* in attendance that occurred at *All Saints, Pawleys* during four of the twenty-three *Murphy Years* were clearly identifiable and known to most of the members.

What was not known in 2005 was whether the growth of the congregation had stabilized, or whether *All Saints, Pawleys* would experience another season of growth when Chuck Murphy's successor, Terrell Glenn became its twenty-first rector and senior pastor.

The Rev. Terrell Lyles Glenn—the Twenty-First Rector of *All Saints, Pawleys*

The Rev. Terrell L. Glenn served as the Rector and Senior Pastor of the largest Episcopal church in the Diocese of South Carolina, *St. Andrews, Mt. Pleasant* for ten years. Glenn left *St. Andrews* and The Episcopal Church to organize a new AMiA church in Raleigh, North Carolina. Glenn's new church, *Church of the Apostles*, was phenomenally successful and had already organized its first daughter church in Chapel Hill, North Carolina when Glenn accepted the call to become the twenty-first rector of *All Saints, Pawleys*.

Filling Chuck Murphy's shoes was a daunting task, but Terrell Glenn was up for the challenge. Glenn served *All Saints, Pawleys* well for five years before becoming a full-time Bishop within the AMiA. Glenn announced his resignation in November 2010; and in January 2011, the Rev. Robert L. Grafe, Jr. was called to be the twenty-second Rector and Senior Pastor of *All Saints, Pawleys*. Grafe had joined the *All Saints, Pawleys* staff a year earlier and had been well received by the membership.

In his farewell message at the Annual Parish Meeting in January 2011, Terrell Glenn humbly disclosed to a packed fellowship hall that all of the churches where had served previously had experienced dramatic growth after his departure. Those in attendance had to wonder whether this pattern would repeat itself at *All Saints, Pawleys*. Many felt that it would, and a sense of eager anticipation and expectation awaited the installation of Rob Grafe as the twenty-second Rector and Senior pastor of *All Saints, Pawleys.*

Practical Applications
of the Model

When Chuck Murphy came to *All Saints, Pawleys*, he had never heard of sociologists of religion Dean Hoge and David Roozen, nor was he aware of their research and conclusions concerning the correlation between *local institutional factors* and congregational growth. Nevertheless, *the eight building blocks of the early church*, the components of the first century worship and leadership model that Chuck Murphy taught and implemented at *All Saints, Pawleys*, produced all ten *local institutional factors* that Hoge and Roozen found to be highly correlated with congregational growth.

The remarkable growth and transformation of *All Saints, Pawleys* during *The Murphy Years* has been well documented. The obvious question that remains is whether the first century worship and leadership model described in this book is transferable—can other local congregations achieve results similar to those realized by *All Saints, Pawleys* by implementing the model?

Can Other Congregations Duplicate the Success of *All Saints, Pawleys* by Implementing the Model?

Chuck Murphy suggested to the pastors and leaders of the sixty-nine congregations who visited *All Saints, Pawleys* during the Visiting Vestry Weekends that they view the first century worship and leadership model as a cafeteria, a smorgasbord, an assortment of tools and ministries that were available for them to pick and choose from. Murphy admonished these leaders not to attempt to duplicate the entire model.

Rather, he suggested that they choose one or two elements of the model to implement initially. Murphy also admitted candidly that some of the elements of the model may not function as effectively in other environments as they had at *All Saints, Pawleys*.

The Rev. David Bryan, pastor of the *Church of St. Luke and St. Peter* in St. Cloud, Florida, a suburb of Orlando, was one of the pastors who brought his Vestry to visit *All Saints, Pawleys*. When asked, Bryan recalled that he and his leadership team were able to successfully implement several elements of the model including the introduction of contemporary music into a blended worship service. Bryan later became Murphy's assistant at *All Saints, Pawleys*; and in 2005, he successfully planted a new AMiA church, *Christ Church, Murrells Inlet,* in nearby Murrells Inlet, South Carolina.

AMiA Bishop T. J. Johnston, another of Murphy's assistants, left *All Saints, Pawleys* to plant a new AMiA church in Little Rock, Arkansas, and another one in Mt. Pleasant, South Carolina. According to Bishop Johnston, both of these congregations implemented successfully many elements of the worship and leadership model that he had helped Chuck Murphy implement at *All Saints, Pawleys*.

The Rev. John Greene who left *All Saints, Pawleys* to plant a new AMiA church in Asheville, North Carolina; and the Rt. Rev. Thaddeus Barnum who left *All Saints, Pawleys* to plant a new AMiA church in Fairfield, Connecticut; and the Rev. David Linka who left *All Saints, Pawleys* to a plant new AMiA church in Petoskey, Michigan and later assumed the leadership of an AMiA congregation in Morehead City, North Carolina, all implemented successfully parts if not all of this worship and leadership model in their congregations.

Therefore, the success of the first century worship and leadership model was not limited to *All Saints, Pawleys* or Pawleys Island, South Carolina. The model has been successfully transferred to other congregations in different parts of the country.

Planting New Churches Versus Revitalizing Existing Churches

In the United States and in the United Kingdom, interest in church planting (organizing new churches) has increased in recent years. Thom Rainer and others have documented that unchurched people are attracted more easily to new churches than to existing ones. However, two factors must be considered before one decides to plant a new church today in the United States or the United Kingdom.

First, the religious landscape in both the United States and the United Kingdom is littered with existing congregations and underutilized church buildings. One English commentator has suggested somewhat facetiously that no more new churches should be organized in England. Rather, half of the existing churches should be closed; so that the remaining ones would be at least half-full on Sunday mornings.

While this suggestion may have some merit, a more effective strategy may be for church planters to utilize those existing church buildings by revitalizing those congregations as Chuck Murphy did in Pawleys Island. *All Saints, Pawleys* was a small 250 year old congregation when Chuck Murphy arrived.

Church planters will respond correctly that it is much more difficult to transform an existing congregation into a new paradigm church than it is to start a new one. Thad Barnum will remind these church planters that Jesus said to take the narrow path, not the wide one. Rick Warren will remind them that God equips His people to accomplish His purposes.

All Saints, Pawleys and the first century worship and leadership model offer particular encouragement to church planters who choose to revitalize existing congregations, especially those within the mainline denominations in the U.S. and the U.K. that are in such desperate need of revival.

The Biggest Challenge For Church Planters Today Is Not To Attract a Crowd

The biggest challenge for church planters today is not to attract a crowd but to acquire affordable land and buildings for that crowd to worship in. The costs of acquiring land and constructing buildings have skyrocketed in the United States and in the United Kingdom.

For example, land in the coastal region of South Carolina that sold for approximately $20,000 per acre in 2005 sold for over $80,000 per acre five years later. A minimum of four acres is required for a typical church plant (church architects suggest one acre per one hundred members). Therefore, the land costs alone for a new church in the United States can easily approach a half million dollars.

Church Property Investors, LLC: An Idea that Every Congregation Should Embrace

In 2002, members of an Acts 2:42 Group at *All Saints, Pawleys* invited evangelist Luis Palau to hold an evangelistic festival in nearby Myrtle Beach— *Beachfest at Broadway with Luis Palau.* Over 80,000 people attended the festival from 16 states and 3 foreign countries. Several unchurched "twenty-somethings" from Myrtle Beach attended this festival and saw the outpouring of the Spirit upon the thousands that were there. These twenty-somethings, most of whom were involved in one way or the other with the real estate business, decided to use their gifts and experience to impact the Myrtle Beach area for Christ.

The members of the group began to pray and ask for discernment about some next steps that they might take. Then, the Holy Spirit revealed to them that they should form a real estate investment company whose sole mission was to acquire land for future church plants. The group organized Church Property Investors, LLC, a real estate investment company and adopted the following as their company logo: *Acquiring Land Today for Churches Tomorrow.*

Several members of the group had access to Multiple Listing data and other sources of information about property that could possibly be used for future church plants. The company soon acquired two tracts of land. The first tract was used by *Christ Church, Murrells Inlet*, discussed above, and a second tract was acquired for *Barefoot Community Church*, a church plant in nearby North Myrtle Beach.

The senior pastor of *Barefoot Community Church,* Clay Nesmith, was also a member of the Acts 2:42 Group that formed Church Property Investors, LLC. The group included three pastors (which was atypical for Acts 2:42 Groups). When Nesmith observed the outpouring of the Spirit at the Luis Palau Festival, God put on his heart to plant a new church in nearby North Myrtle Beach.

Five years later, *Barefoot Community Church*, a non-denominational, evangelical, community church had an average Sunday attendance of 2,400. Its attendance was much greater than *All Saints, Pawleys*, but it would not have existed if Clay Nesmith had not been a member of that *All Saints, Pawleys'* Acts 2:42 Group that helped organize the Luis Palau Festival and later formed Church Property Investors, LLC. Once again, *All Saints, Pawleys* had lived into its Vision Statement: to share the Full Counsel of God with the whole Church and the World.

Are Certain Areas More Fertile for Church Plants?

Research by Thom Rainer and others has shown conclusively that newcomers are the most effective targets for church planters. Prior to planting Saddleback Community Church, Rick Warren spent months in the library pouring over census data in order to locate the fastest growing community of the fastest growing county of the fastest growing state in the country. Today, all of this data is available to church planters at www.census.gov.

Therefore, church planters should not look for areas with the largest population. Rather, they should identify areas with the largest *increases* in population. Technical analysts who evaluate investments have found that trends in place tend to stay in place. The same axiom applies to population growth. Therefore, church planters need to identify areas where the population is growing the fastest like the cities and counties shown in the tables that follow.

The Fastest Growing Cities in Each State

1. Smiths, Alabama	26. Kalispell, Montana
2. Anchorage, Alaska	27. Bellevue, Nebraska
3. Buckeye, Arizona	28. Summerlin South, Nevada
4. Conway, Arkansas	29. Derry, New Hampshire
5. Lincoln, California	30. Hoboken, New Jersey
6. Black Forest, Colorado	31. Rio Rancho, New Mexico
7. Shelton, Connecticut	32. White Plains, New York
8. Wilmington, Delaware	33. Wake Forest, North Carolina
9. Fruit Cove, Florida	34. Fargo, North Dakota
10. Braselton, Georgia	35. Dublin, Ohio
11. Pearl City, Hawaii	36. Edmond, Oklahoma
12. Meridian, Ohio	37. Hillsboro, Oregon
13. Northbrook, Illinois	38. Back Mountain, Pennsylvania
14. Avon, Indiana	39. Cranston, Rhode Island
15. Urbandale, Iowa	40. Fort Mill, South Carolina
16. Leawood, Kansas	41. Sioux Falls, South Dakota
17. Nicholasville, Kentucky	42. Spring Hill, Tennessee
18. Houma, Louisiana	43. Atcosita, Texas
19. South Portland, Maine	44. South Jordan, Utah
20. North Bethesda, Maryland	45. Burlington, Vermont
21. Lexington, Massachusetts	46. McLean, Virginia
22. Plymouth Township, Michigan	47. Seattle Hills-Silver Firs, Washington
23. Maple Grove, Minnesota	48. Martinsburg, West Virginia
24. South Haven, Mississippi	49. Neenah, Wisconsin
25. Lee's Summit, Missouri	50. Gillette, Wyoming

**Source: Bloomberg Businessweek;
see also: census.gov.**

**Ten Fastest Growing Counties and Cities in
the United States Since 2000**

Counties	Cities
1. Kendall County, Illinois	1. New Orleans, Louisiana
2. Pinal County, Arizona	2. Round Rock, Texas
3. Rockwall, Texas	3. Cary, North Carolina
4. Loudon County, Virginia	4. Gilbert, Arizona
5. Flagler County, Florida	5. McKinney, Texas
6. Forsyth County, Georgia	6. Roseville, California
7. Paulding County, Georgia	7. Irvine, California
8. Lincoln County, South Dakota	8. Raleigh, North Carolina
9. Williamson County, Texas	9. Killeen, Texas
10. Douglas County, Colorado	10. Fort Worth, Texas

Source: United States Census Bureau: Census.gov.

Exploding the Myth: Retirement Communities Are Fertile Ground for Church Planters

Volumes have been written about the *graying* of America and the United Kingdom. In the year 2000, 35 million Americans were 65 and older. By the year 2020, that number is expected to reach 54 million and more than double again by the year 2050. In order to provide affordable and maintenance free housing for this abundance of retirees, retirement communities, virtual cities for retirees, are being developed throughout the United States and the United Kingdom.

However, a myth exists in the United States (and presumably in the United Kingdom), that it is more difficult to get older, more educated, and affluent people to attend church regularly. Chuck Murphy exploded this myth by creating an environment at *All Saints, Pawleys* where people (especially those over 65) could experience the living God. According to Murphy, older people, regardless of their education and affluence, long for community, fellowship, and transcendence. They have the time and the inclination to experience the living God; and they often have the resources to invest in God's agenda. Therefore, retirement communities are fertile ground for new church plants.

According to the *All Saints, Pawleys'* membership survey, over 50 percent of the members that regularly attended *All Saints, Pawleys* were over the age of sixty-five. Therefore, Murphy and the first century worship and leadership model that he implemented were extremely effective at reaching this segment of the population that has been largely overlooked by church planters.

Another prevailing myth is that young couples with children do not live in retirement communities. The studies of congregations discussed in this book revealed a direct correlation between congregational growth and the number of young couples with children in the home. When Chuck Murphy became the senior pastor of *All Saints, Pawleys,* very few young couples with children in the home lived in Pawleys Island. However, as the number of retirees increased, the demand for support services increased. Doctors, nurses, lawyers, accountants, golf course attendants, waiters and waitresses, and the like, many with young children in the home, moved into Pawleys Island.

<u>Gated Communities Are Virtual Cities Without</u>
<u>Churches—Manna From Heaven for Church Planters</u>

During the colonial era of the United States, most villages had at least three churches: a Congregational church, a Presbyterian church, and an Anglican church. Today in the United States, large gated communities—virtual cities—typically have no churches. These communities are manna from heaven for prospective church planters.

A huge pent-up demand exists in these often densely populated communities for new paradigm churches like *All Saints, Pawleys*, churches that offer multiple services—traditional services for the retirees and more contemporary services for the young couples with children. The phenomenal success at *All Saints, Pawleys* of the "blended" and the "contemporary" services proved conclusively that both retirees and young couples with children in the home can and will worship at the same church—provided that they experience the living God when they attend. Prospective church planters should identify and target nearby gated communities as potential sites for church plants.

Therefore, practical applications of the first century worship and leadership model described in this book abound. What is needed is pastors, church planters, and lay-leaders who will take this model and run with it. God has given us the blueprints to re-build His Church. Use them for his Glory!

CONCLUSION

A More Effective Worship and Leadership Model is Needed to Equip Churches for the Next Reformation

The Next Reformation and the First Century Worship and Leadership Model

According to Kevin Donlon, an Oxford-trained historian and distinguished canon lawyer, the Christian church has undergone significant reformations at five hundred year intervals since its inception. The first reform movement, Monasticism, began in the fifth century following the fall of Rome when the church was forced to go underground into the monasteries of Europe. However, as Monasticism preserved and strengthened the church, very different spiritualities and politics emerged in the common life of the Empire that resulted in the great break between the Eastern Orthodox and the Roman Catholic churches in 1054.

The culture and society of Western Europe flourished for a time, but markers became apparent that more change was coming. The minds of the people had become darkened with superstition, ignorance, and bigotry. As the amount of information increased (via the printing press), an increase in dissatisfaction with the prevailing religious conditions brought about a third reformation.

According to Donlon, we now find ourselves poised for the next reformation as the church moves into the 21st century in a state of transition amidst a profound sense of fragmentation.[1] Eddie Gibbs and Rick Warren agree with Donlon. In fact, both of them have declared that the next Reformation has already begun! So the question is: Will the Protestant church in the United States and the United Kingdom rise to the occasion?

Do the pastors and leaders of local congregations have a proven and effective worship and leadership model in place that will sustain the church through the ominous challenges that lie ahead? According to the social scientists, theologians, and church growth experts, local congregations in the United States and the United Kingdom are not equipped for the battle.

These experts have concluded that local congregations need a more effective worship and leadership model. This book has presented such a model—a proven model—not a theory, but an actual model that was implemented successfully in the first century church and has been implemented successfully in several twenty-first century churches, including *All Saints, Pawleys.*

The remarkable growth and transformation that occurred at *All Saints, Pawleys* can occur in any congregation where the pastors and leaders of the congregation implement this first century model, if the pastors and leaders expect transformation to occur.

An Attitude of Expectation

William Carey, one of the first missionaries to China, once said: "If we attempt great things *for* God, we can *expect* great things *from* God." In *The Mind of Jesus*, William Barclay said: "We might well receive more miracles, if we stopped insisting that miracles do not happen, and began *expecting* them to happen."

In his opening address to the 11th annual AMiA Winter Conference, Chuck Murphy told 1,400 Anglicans from 36 states and 6 countries that they should have an *attitude of expectation*. Murphy added that throughout his 35 years of ordained ministry he had *expected* God to do great things, and that God always had. Murphy challenged the group to develop a *Christ-centered expectation*. "God is already here," Murphy exhorted: "Join Him!"

A Final Challenge

Echoing Chuck Murphy's words, I feel compelled to issue this final challenge. An effective and proven worship and leadership model already exists, the first century model that has been described in this book. See it. Seize it. Shout it from the rooftops! Then get out of the way, and let God bring growth and transformation to your congregation. Expect it to occur, and it will!

ACKNOWLEDGEMENTS

I would like to express my utmost gratitude to Bishop Chuck Murphy, Chairman of the *Anglican Mission in the Americas*, for his godly counsel during my *second-half* journey and for allowing me to describe, for the first time in print, the components of the worship and leadership model that he implemented with great success at *All Saints, Pawleys*.

A church planter studying at the *Institute for Christian Leadership* once asked Chuck Murphy if he could use some of his hand-outs. Without hesitation, Murphy replied: "Go ahead, rip me off! I didn't invent this stuff, God did. Use it for His glory!" Encouragement like this was an every day occurrence at *All Saints, Pawleys* during *The Murphy Years*.

I also want to express my gratitude to my professors and mentors who both inspired me and encouraged me to write this book: Dr. James L. Skinner, Professor of English at Presbyterian College (retired); Dr. Philip W. Comfort, Dean of the Institute for Christian Leadership and Senior Editor, Tyndale House Publishers; Dr. William A. Jones, President, Columbia International University; Dr. Derek Tidball, Principal (Retired), London School of Theology; Dr. Norman Doe, Director of the Centre of Law and Religion, Cardiff University

Law School; Dr. Linus Morris, President, Christian Associates International; Dr. Dwight Smith, President, Saturation Church Planting International; Dr. Joel Comiskey, President, The Joel Comiskey Group; Mike Breen, President, 3D Ministries; Lloyd Reeb, President, Half-Time, Inc.; and B. Larkin Spivey, author and retired U.S. Marine. These godly men have inspired me and encouraged me greatly during my *second-half journey from empire building to Kingdom building.*

Finally, I would like to thank Dr. Luis Palau, Dr. James I. Packer, Canon Malcolm Widdecombe, the Rt. Rev. FitzSimmons Allison, Bishop of South Carolina (retired), and the Rt. Rev. Alex Dickson, Bishop of West Tennessee (retired). If more servants of God were willing to embrace the *faith once delivered to the Saints*, as these men have done tirelessly throughout their lives, no crisis of faith and leadership would exist within the church today.

To God be the glory for the lives of all of these servant leaders and for their work for the Kingdom.

Ross Lindsay

APPENDIX 1

The Research Methodology

The research for this book applied the same "interpretative framework" to *All Saints, Pawleys* that Hoge and Roozen applied to sixteen different denominations and over six hundred congregations in their landmark study, *Understanding Church Growth and Decline.* Their interpretative framework included four categories of analysis:

(1) National Contextual Factors: forces operating at a national level, external to the church
(2) National Institutional Factors: forces internal to the church, but whose control was at the national level
(3) Local Contextual Factors: characteristics of the local community, over which the local congregations had no control
(4) Local Institutional Factors: forces internal to the local church, which could encourage or dissuade membership and participation

Hoge and Roozen's study concluded that the consistent declines in membership and attendance within the mainline denominational churches in the United States could be accounted for by "National Contextual Factors." The *All Saints, Pawleys'* study concluded that the consistent growth in membership and attendance within *All Saints, Pawleys* could be accounted for by "Local Institutional Factors" that were imbedded in its unique worship and leadership model.

As part of the research, a survey of the members of *All Saints, Pawleys* was conducted in November 2005. A questionnaire was disseminated while families were waiting to have their photo taken for the church directory. 510 members or 77 percent of the members of the congregation completed and returned the questionnaire. Excerpts and conclusions from the data gathered in the surveys is presented in relevant places of the text; however the complete questionnaire and a summary of the responses follow as Appendix 2.

Appendix 2

The *All Saints, Pawleys'* Membership Survey

1. Which worship service do you usually attend?
   - a. 8:00 a.m. Traditional   (T)   38
   - b. 9:30 a.m. Blended   (B)   249
   - c. 9:30 a.m. Access   (A)   166
   - d. 10:30 a.m. ECUSA   (E)   21
   - e. 10:00 a.m. Wednesday   2
   - f. Multiple services   34
   -     Total Respondents   510

2. When were you born?

	T	B	A	E	Total	Pct
a. 1910-1919	4	3	0	3	10	1.9%
b. 1920-1929	11	25	2	6	48	9.4%
c. 1930-1939	13	75	8	5	108	21.1%
d. 1940-1949	6	75	20	5	116	22.7%
e. 1950-1959	4	29	29	2	73	14.3%
f. 1960-1969		28	50		81	15.8%
g. 1970-1979		9	40		52	10.1%
h. 1980-1989		3	14		17	3.3%
i. 1990-1999		2	3		5	1.4%

3. Where were you born?

	T	B	A	E	Total	Pct
South Carolina	4	82	65	9	181	35.4%
North Carolina	3	25	17	2	50	9.8%
New York	4	19	12		35	7.0%
Pennsylvania	2	10	14		29	5.7%
Ohio	2	6	6	1	18	3.5%
Illinois	1	7	6		15	2.9%
New Jersey	2	7	4	1	14	2.7%
Virginia		7	2	3	13	2.5%
Florida		6	5		11	2.2%
Georgia	3	7	1		11	2.2%
Tennessee	1	8	1		11	2.2%
Wash., DC	1	4	2		8	1.6%
Massachusetts		5	3		8	1.6%
Indiana		5	2		7	1.4%
Canada		2	4	1	7	1.4%
Other Places	25	44	25	4	91	17.8%

4. Where did you live before moving to Pawleys Island?

	T	B	A	E	Total	Pct
South Carolina	4	87	78	7	191	37.4%
North Carolina	5	40	15	1	65	12.7%
Georgia	3	9	7	1	23	4.5%
Florida	2	5	11	1	20	3.9%
New Jersey	6	5	6		19	3.7%
Pennsylvania	1	11	6		19	3.7%
Virginia	2	12	4		19	3.7%
Tennessee	2	9		2	14	2.7%
Ohio		8	4		12	2.3%
Maryland	4	5	1	1	12	2.3%
New York	1	9	1		11	2.2%
Massachusetts		4	4		9	1.8%
Indiana	1	3	4		8	1.6%
Texas		6		1	8	1.6%
Illinois	1	4	1		7	1.4%
Michigan		4	3		7	1.4%
Connecticut	1	5			6	1.2%
25 Other Places	6	21	13		49	9.6%

5. How often did you attend church as a child?

	T	B	A	E	Total	Pct
a. Several times a week	4	37	23		72	14.1%
b. Every week	29	163	89	18	320	62.7%
c 2-3 times a month	2	27	27	1	61	11.9%
d. Several times a year	2	16	16	1	36	7.1%
e. Once or twice a year		1	4		6	1.2%
f. Rarely, if ever		4	5	1	11	2.1%
g. Don't remember	1	1	2		4	.9%

6. What denomination was the church that you attended as a child?

	T	B	A	E	Total	Pct
Episcopal (Anglican)	13	57	38	10	129	23.5%
Baptist	6	51	22	3	90	17.6%
Methodist	5	46	31	3	88	17.2%
Presbyterian	3	31	20	1	63	12.4%
Roman Catholic	4	28	21		57	11.2%
Lutheran	4	14	11		30	5.9%
Non-denominational	2	7	6	4	19	3.7%
Congregational (UCoC)	1	5	4		10	2.0%
Unchurched		3	6		9	1.8%
Pentecostal		3	4		7	1.4%
Other		4	3		8	1.6%

7. What was the denomination of the church that you attended before transferring to All Saints, Pawleys?

	T	B	A	E	Total	Pct
Episcopal (Anglican)	29	98	44	15	202	39.6%
Presbyterian	3	44	15	1	72	14.1%
Methodist	1	29	22	1	54	10.6%
Baptist		26	17	1	46	9.0%
Unchurched	2	9	22		35	6.9%
Roman Catholic		12	19		33	6.5%
Non-denominational	1	15	15	1	33	6.5%
Lutheran		11	5		17	3.3%
Congregational (UCC)	2	3	4		10	2.0%
Pentecostal (AoG)		2	3		6	1.2%

8. What is the highest level of education that you completed?

	T	B	A	E	Total	Pct
High School	5	33	31	2	74	15.1%
College	19	147	87	9	274	56.0%
Graduate or Professional School	13	68	43	10	134	20.4%
No answer	1	1	5		7	8.5%

9. What first attracted you to All Saints, Pawleys?

(Rank 1-6)	T	B	A	E	Total
Preaching	1	1	1	2	5
Fellowship (Community)	2	2	2	1	7
Teaching	3	3	4	3	13
Music	4	4	3	6	17
Lay Ministries	5	5	5	4	19
Counseling	6	6	6	5	23

10. How long have you attended All Saints, Pawleys?

	T	B	A	E	Total	Pct
More than 15 years	16	71	23	11	137	27.0%
1-3 years	9	45	54	1	113	22.3%
7-10 years	4	50	28	1	92	18.0%
4-6 years	1	45	35	1	86	17.0%
11-15 years	7	31	18	58	11.5%	
Less than one year	1	6	7	5	20	4.2%

11. How often do you attend All Saints, Pawleys?

	T	B	A	E	Total	Pct
Usually once each week.	25	161	108	13	322	63.1%
More than once each week.	9	72	14		114	22.3%
2-3 times a month.	4	11	31	2	53	10.4%
Usually once each month		2	7		9	1.8%
2 -3 times each year		3	3	2	8	1.6%
Don't attend anymore				4	4	.8%

12. How far do you travel to attend All Saints, Pawleys?

	T	B	A	E	Total	Pct
1-3 miles	27	144	78	14	286	56.1%
3-5 miles	9	42	41	2	100	19.6%
11-15 miles		23	29	2	60	11.7%
6-10 miles		17	8	1	28	5.5%
16-25 miles	2	15	7		28	5.5%
More than 25 miles		7	1		8	1.6%

13. Do you believe in the existence of?

		T	B	A	E	Total	Pct
Heaven?	Yes	35	248	163	20	500	98.6%
	No	0				0	
	Not Sure	3	1	2	1	7	1.4%
Hell?	Yes	28	233	153	10	447	91.9%
	No	2	4	3		9	1.8%
	Not Sure	8	12	9	11	30	6.3%
The Satan)?	Devil (or						
	Yes	26	237	153	14	461	90.9%
	No	1	4	5	2	13	2.5%
	Not Sure	11	8	7	5	33	6.6%
Demons?	Yes	11	186	104	6	331	65.3%
	No	12	22	24	7	65	12.8%
	Not Sure	15	41	37	8	111	21.9%
Miracles?	Yes	33	240	153	20	478	94.3%
	No	1	1	2		4	.7%
	Not Sure	4	8	10	1	25	5.0%

14. Do you believe that the Bible is __?

	T	B	A	E	Total	Pct
God breathed, the actual word of God that is to be taken literally.	17	173	97	3	320	62.7%
The inspired word of God that was recorded by men and should not always be taken literally.	15	68	54	14	156	30.6%
Truth and wisdom that applied to the early church but must be re-interpreted today in light of our scientificknowledge and cultural context		2	1		4	.8%
Composed of history and moral precepts that were inspired by men.	5	2	7	2	16	3.1%
e. No answer	1	4	7	2	14	2.8%

15. Who goes to heaven?

	T	B	A	E	Total	Pct
Only those people who accept Jesus as their personal Savior	31	234	140	11	444	87.0%
People who love others and do good things	6	7	15	5	35	6.8%
Everyone	1	5	8		15	2.9%
People who go to church regularly		1			1	.4%
Not sure/No Answer	4	2	3	5	15	2.9%

16. How often do you pray?

	T	B	A	E	Total	Pct
Several times a day	21	192	93	10	350	68.6%
Once a day	8	25	38	6	80	15.7%
Several times a week	7	22	24	4	58	11.4%
Once a week	1	4	6		11	2.2%
Several times a year	1	1			2	.4%
Rarely if ever/No answer		5	3	1	9	1.7%

17. How often do you read the Bible?

	T	B	A	E	Total	Pct
Every day	10	110	26	3	169	33.1%
2-3 times each week	8	83	53	4	155	30.4%
Rarely, if ever	9	17	37	4	72	14.1%
2-3 times each month	7	20	35	3	69	13.5%
2-3 times each year	3	12	13	4	32	6.3%
No answer	1	7	2	3	13	2.5%

18. If you were ill or faced with a difficult situation, how much assistance and comfort would you expect the people of All Saints, Pawleys to give you?

	T	B	A	E	Total	Pct
Whatever assistance I needed without my having to ask for it	12	90	33	6	153	30.0%
Some assistance without my having to ask for it	16	64	48	3	143	28.0%
Whatever assistance that I asked for	4	64	55	4	134	26.3%
Some assistance but only if I asked if I asked for it.	5	20	15	3	49	9.6%
No answer	1	11	13	5	31	6.1%

19. Do you believe God actually hears and answers your prayers?

	T	B	A	E	Total	Pct
Yes definitely	24	213	130	15	415	81.4%
Yes	10	28	28	4	73	14.3%
No	1		2		3	.6%
Not sure/no answer	3	8	6	2	19	6.7%

20. Has there ever been a turning point in your life when you made a new and personal commitment or re-commitment to Jesus Christ as your personal Savior?

	T	B	A	E	Total	Pct
Yes	18	207	125	6	387	75.9%
No	10	2	11	4	28	5.5%
I don't recall a specific time.	10	40	30	9	93	18.2%
No answer	2		2			.4%

21. Do you feel that you actually experience or encounter God when you worship at this church?

	T	B	A	E	Total	Pct
Yes, every week.	18	151	76	5	271	53.1%
Yes, often but not every week.	14	69	67	5	168	32.9%
Yes, but not as much as I once did.		14	5		21	4.1%
Not very often	1	5	10	3	19	3.7%
No	5	2	1	1	9	1.7%
No answer		8	7	7	22	4.5%

22. How did you find out about All Saints, Pawleys?

	T	B	A	Total	Pct
Recommended by a friend.	11	108	79	213	41.8%
Recommended by a family member	6	48	56	114	22.4%
Born into Episcopal Church	4	16	6	31	6.1%
Other					29.7%

The following were given as other ways parishioners discovered All Saints, Pawleys:

Summer visits to Pawleys	5	13	2	21
Closest church	4	9	2	17
Visited and came back	1	9	2	15
Just drove by it	4	1	1	6
Women in Discipleship		1	4	6
Other Episcopal churches	1	3	1	6
Newspaper ads		4		5
All Saints School		2	2	5
Cursillo		2	1	3
Wednesday service		3		3
Hired as staff member		1	2	
Website		2		2

Newcomer's Letter		1	1	2
Realtor	2			2
All Saints Arts Series		1		1
Alpha Class		1		1
Bible Study at Curves			1	1
Sign on Highway 17	1			1
Thad Barnum's Preaching		1		1
Attending a wedding		1		1
Yellow Pages		1		1
Youth Ministry		1		1
Moved to Pawleys		1		1
Just fell in the door		1		1
Unspecified	1	15	7	24

23. What do you think that All Saints, Pawleys does best today? (Rank from 1 to 6 with 1 being the best)

	T	B	A	E	Total
____ Preaching	1.31	1.30	1.72	1.27	1.428
____ Teaching	1.46	2.76	2.94	n/a	2.766
____ Friendliness of Members	1.70	3.29	3.25	1.54	3.128
____ Music	2.86	3.75	3.24	3.70	3.511
____ Lay ministries and programs	2.33	3.80	3.99	n/a	3.869
____ Counseling	2.33	4.81	4.72	3.00	4.682

Notes

Chapter 1: Introduction

1. Factfinder.census.gov/serviet/SAFFPopulation (accessed February 19, 2011).
2. Eileen W. Lindner, *Yearbook of American & Canadian Churches* (Nashville, TN: Abingdon Press, 2011), 10.
3. George Barna, *Re-Churching the Unchurched* (Ventura, CA: Issachar Resources, 2000), 12.

Chapter 2: The State of the Church: A Crisis of Faith and Leadership

1. Jeffrey Hadden,*The Gathering Storm in the Churches* (Garden City, NY: Doubleday, 1969).
2. Peter Brierley (ed.), *UK Christian Handbook, Religious Trends: Nos. 1-5* (London, UK: Christian Research, 2005/2006), 2.23.
3. C. Parkinson and C. Hawkins, *Reveal: Where are You?* (Chicago, IL: Willow Creek Community Church, 2007).
4. Donald Miller, *Reinventing American Protestantism: Christianity in the New Millennium* (Los Angeles, CA: University of California Press, 1997), 183.
5. Miller, 47.

6. Todd Hunter, *The Accidental Anglican* (Downers Grove, IL: IVP, 2010).

7. Eddie Gibbs, *ChurchNext* (Downers Grove, IL: InterVarsity Press, 2000), 72-73.

8. Gibbs, 238.

9. Dave Shiflett, *Exodus: Why Americans are Fleeing Liberal Churches for Conservative Christianity* (New York, NY: Penguin Group, 2005), 83.

Chapter 3: Four Recent Studies Confirm the Need for a Different Model

1. Dean Hoge and David Roozen. *Understanding Church Growth and Decline: 1950-1978* (New York, NY: Pilgrim Press, 1979).

2. Mark Chaves, *Congregations in America* (Cambridge, MA: Harvard University Press, 2004).

3. Cynthia Woolever and Deborah Bruce, *A Field Guide to U.S. Congregations* (Louisville, KY: John Knox Press, 2002).

4. Jim Collins, *Good to Great: Why Some Companies Make the Leap and Others Don't* (New York, NY: Harper Collins Publishers, 2001), 219-227.

5. Thom Rainer, *Breakout Churches* (Grand Rapids, MI: Zondervan, 2005).

6. Thom Rainer, *Surprising Insights From the Unchurched and How to Reach Them* (Grand Rapids, MI: Zondervan, 2001), 223.

7. Thom Rainer and Ed Stetzer, *Transformational Church, Creating a New Scorecard for Congregations* (Nashville, TN: B&H Publishing Group, 2010), 27-29.

8. Rainer and Stetzer, 30.

Chapter 4: Chuck Murphy:
The Man and The Model

1. Field notes from a visit to Pip 'n' Jay in July 2005.
2. Carl George, *How to Break Growth Barriers* (Grand Rapids, MI: Baker Academic Books, 1993), 19.
3. Bob Slosser, *Miracle in Darien* (Plainfield, NJ: Logos International, 1979), 27.

Chapter 5: The Word is Proclaimed

1. Martyn Lloyd-Jones, *Preaching & Preachers* (Grand Rapids, MI: Zondervan, 1971), 9.

Chapter 6: The Need is Acknowledged

1. Field notes from a visit to a Sunday evening worship and healing service at the Toronto Airport Fellowship in July 2002.

Chapter 7: Baptism

1. Martin Stringer, *A Sociological History of Christian Worship* (Cambridge, UK: Cambridge University Press, 2005), 55-56.

Chapter 8: The Apostles's Teaching, Fellowship, and the Eucharist

1. George, *How to Break Growth Barriers,* 188-189.
2. Joel Comiskey, *Cell Church Solutions* (Houston, TX: Touch Publications, 2005).

Chapter 9: Miracles, Awe, and Power

1. John Gunstone, *Pentecostal Anglicans* (London, UK: Hoddey and Stoughton, 1982), 17-18.
2. Peter Mallon, *Calling a City Back to God* (Eastbourne, UK: Kingsway, 2003), 25.
3. William Barclay, *The Mind of Jesus* (San Francisco, CA: HarperSanFrancisco, 1960,1961), 70.

Chapter 10: Stewardship

1. *All Saints, Pawleys Annual Reports: 1982, 2002* (Pawleys Island, SC: All Saints, Pawleys).
2. Lindner, *2005 Yearbook*, 12.
3. Mark Chaves and Sharon Miller, *Financing American Religion* (London, UK: Alta Mira Press, 1999), 37.
4. Chaves and Miller, 40, 44.

Chapter 11: Worship

1. Donald Miller, *Reinventing American Protestantism: Christianity in the New Millennium* (Los Angeles, CA: University of California Press, 1997), 87.
2. Miller, 87.
3. Daniel Albrecht, *Rites in the Spirit* (Sheffield, UK: Sheffield Academic Press, 1999), 239.
4. John Maxwell, *Failing Forward* (Nashville, TN: Thomas Nelson, Inc., 2000).
5. Philip Jenkins, *The Next Christendom* (Oxford, UK: Oxford University Press, 2002), 139.
6. Harvey Cox, *Fire From Heaven* (Cambridge, MA: Da Capo Press, 1995), 312.

Chapter 12: Growth

1. Christian Schwarz, *Natural Church Development* (Carol Stream, IL: ChurchSmart Resources, 1996), 45.
2. Roger Finke and Rodney Stark, *The Churching of America: 1776-1999* (New Brunswick, NJ: Rutgers University Press, 1992), 1.

Chapter 13: Practical Applications of the Model

None

Conclusion

1. Kevin Donlon, *A Three-Fold Cord Not Quickly Broken: An Annotated Catechism for Anglicanism* (Edward Mellen Press, 2006), 44-46.

CPSIA information can be obtained at www.ICGtesting.com
Printed in the USA
LVOW12s1922170414

382150LV00001B/119/P